The Ministry
of Nostalgia

Owen Hatherley

VERSO
London • New York

This paperback edition first published by Verso 2017
First published by Verso 2016
© Owen Hatherley 2016, 2017
Photographs © Owen Hatherley 2016, 2017

3 5 7 9 10 8 6 4 2

Verso
UK: 6 Meard Street, London W1F 0EG
US: 20 Jay Street, Suite 1010, Brooklyn, NY 11201
versobooks.com

Verso is the imprint of New Left Books

ISBN-13: 978-1-78478-076-0
ISBN-13: 978-1-78478-077-7 (UK EBK)
ISBN-13: 978-1-78478-078-4 (US EBK)

British Library Cataloguing in Publication Data
A catalogue record for this book is available from the British Library

The Library of Congress Has Cataloged the Hardback Edition as Follows:

Names: Hatherley, Owen, author.
Title: The ministry of nostalgia : consuming austerity / Owen Hatherley.
Description: London ; Brooklyn, NY : Verso, 2016.
Identifiers: LCCN 2015033877 | ISBN 9781784780753 (hardback)
Subjects: LCSH: Nostalgia–Great Britain. | Great
  Britain–Civilization–1945- | Great Britain–History–20th century. |
  Great Britain–Social conditions–1945- | BISAC: HISTORY / Europe / Great
  Britain.
Classification: LCC DA589.4 .H3735 2016 | DDC 941.085–dc23
LC record available at http://lccn.loc.gov/2015033877

Typeset in Fournier by MJ & N Gavan, Truro, Cornwall
Printed and bound by CPI Group (UK) Ltd, Croydon, CR0 4YY

Contents

Introduction
The Junk Market of Austerity

THE MINISTRY OF NOSTALGIA: We will remind people of how good things used to be. Since no one can now remember a time when things were good, we all need help to dream of a wonderful bygone age when everyone was paid in golden sovereigns, no one was ill or died, the weather was perfect, and you could get 200 pints of bitter for a quid.

Monster Raving Loony Party Manifesto, 1997[1]

In the British General Election of May 2015, 37 percent of registered voters who bothered to turn out voted for austerity. Given that the Conservative–Liberal Democrat government had, for the previous five years, been quite dramatic in the sweep and scale of its policies, perhaps even the most radical government since Thatcher, there's no question of what was being voted for. In education, tuition fees were put up by 300 percent, arts funding was cut by 100 percent; elitist free schools and privately run Academies were expanded; the Education Maintenance Allowance that kept many working-class children in further education was abolished. In housing, a 'bedroom tax' was introduced that was expressly designed to force poor people out of homes deemed 'too large' for them, lifelong tenure in social housing was abolished and in 'Help to Buy', handouts were offered to mount the property ladder instead. In the National Health Service, a Health and Social Care Bill was introduced that opened up most of the NHS to private companies; benefit cuts and punitive benefit sanctions led to millions using food banks; what new jobs emerged were usually on 'zero hours' contracts, the sort of working conditions last seen on nineteenth-century dockland. The privatisation of the railways was reinforced, with the East Coast Line sold to Virgin, and the banks nationalised at the height of the financial crisis were allowed to continue much as before, albeit lending somewhat less. All of this, however, made little dent in the allegedly terrifying national deficit. That 37 percent was a straightforward endorsement for the government's continued attack on the poor.

Although the vote of May 2015 was not some Thatcher-era swell of Tory support, something in this austerity agenda nonetheless struck a chord with people. At the same time Labour, under the hapless leadership of Edward Miliband, offered no serious opposition to austerity as either concept or policy, preferring instead the comically innocuous criticism that the carve-up of the welfare state's few remnants went 'too far, too fast'.

The rhetoric of the opposition to austerity, such as it was, was communitarian and traditional. The irony, however, was palpable. What cultures of opposition did emerge during this time – particularly after a brief flurry of protest in 2011 collapsed in repression and defeat – were deeply indebted to a nostalgic rhetoric of a former period of austerity, just as they attempted to formulate a feasible resistance to its contemporary incarnation.

This failure to articulate the differences between the past and the present condition was only too clear. In March 2013, the filmmaker Ken Loach released a documentary about the last era of 'austerity', *The Spirit of '45*. At the same time, Loach was involved in the foundation of a new left-wing political party, Left Unity, seemingly set on the rock of that spirit. But what do these two moments in history actually have in common?

The period of 'post-war austerity' entailed, as well as rationing and a certain cultural puritanism, the construction of a welfare state, the creation of generous state benefits and the building of a comprehensive system of health care and education, alongside collective bargaining with strong trade unions, the guarantee of full employment, and a massive public housing programme. Meanwhile the 'austerity' of the Coalition government entailed destroying all of these and replacing them with little but scorched earth. Here, the future, if it was thought about at all, was primed to resemble an enterprise zone full of call centres on the edge of a business park on the M4. So how has it been possible to invoke the 1940s in defence of the 2010s?

'Austerity Britain', the period roughly from the 1940s until around 1955, when rationing was finally lifted by a Conservative government, is the direct opposite of

'Austerity Britain' Mark Two, the period from 2009/10 until the present when a financial crisis caused by property speculation and 'derivatives' culminated in massive state bailouts of the largest banks, followed by an assault on what remained of the public sphere after thirty years of neoliberalism. But this most recent austerity has nonetheless been overlaid with the imagery of that earlier era. At times this has been so pervasive that it felt as if parts of the country began to resemble a strange, dreamlike reconstruction of the 1940s and 1950s, reassembled in the wrong order.

A couple of weeks after the election, I chanced upon a market being held on a bank holiday weekend, in Greenwich, South-East London. In front of the Cutty Sark, a late-nineteenth-century tea clipper whose dry dock had recently been encased in faceted glass and the ship hoisted into the air in renovation so poorly considered that it won the 2012 Carbuncle Cup for the Ugliest Building in the UK, were a variety of stalls selling things. Here one could rummage through wartime memorabilia – old tins, plates, tat of various sorts. Another stall was selling records but stocked nothing beyond about 1965. The fashion on display: for men, moustaches and beards, sensible utility wear; for women, the semi-ironic sexualised style usually called 'burlesque'. And looming over everything, the ubiquitous poster demanding that you

KEEP CALM
AND
CARRY ON

Tesco, Woolwich, May 2015

The effect was as if pop music and the social revolutions of the 1960s – the struggles for sexual equality, and particularly, racial equality – had never happened. Instead, everyone had decided to live in their own customised pre-liberation era.

I have seen this market, and places like it, proliferate since around 2008, but encountering it so soon after the electoral victory of austerity made it especially uncomfortable. Not because I suspected these people had actually gone out and voted for five more years of suffering – in fact, given that the Labour vote went up significantly in London, they were less likely to have done so than anyone else. What was depressing was more the dominance of a certain 'structure of feeling' (to use Raymond Williams's phrase), where austerity's look, its historical syncretism, its rejection of the real human advances of the post-war era had seeped into the consciousness of people who would, when pressed, probably be in opposition to it, even as they performed its aesthetics.

Nobody in the actual austerity era would ever have really looked like this. The combination of rockabilly and school-teacher was not, in fact, a common one; but that's really not important. 'Retrochic', as the Marxist cultural historian Raphael Samuel claimed in his 1994 study *Theatres of Memory*, steals from the past at random. This was what distinguished it from the sententiousness of 'heritage'.

In contrast to my anxiousness about the contents of the stalls in Greenwich, Samuel began his book – a defence of heritage culture against its many adversaries on the left – with a survey of the wares for sale at Camden Market. For him, this activity prompted a speculation on the way discarded waste products had been transformed from emergency salvage to desirable consumer items. He also spotted that many contemporary record covers no longer presented an image of futurism, or an optimistic present, but – as seen in the aesthetics of The Smiths and Billy Bragg – absconded into a more repressed, provincial Britain of the pre-pop years, when desires were not to be instantly satisfied.[2]

Samuel's argument was that 'retrochic' and various other popular uses of the past offered something that dry historical accounts could not. They offered a haptic experience of the past that you could smell, touch and experience; one that was democratic, where no special knowledge was necessary, but was nonetheless populated by amateur enthusiasts and obsessives. This was something to celebrate, not a reason for snark.

Retrochic, he claimed, seemed to differ from earlier forms of revival, partly because of the lack of sentimentality that it held for the past. Instead, its energies were fixed on 'animating the inanimate'.[3] Before retrochic, born at the moment when youth in the post-war Elephant and Castle started wearing aristocratic Edwardian clothes – 'Teddy Boys' – revivals were top-down affairs.[4] But as the retro-culture of Camden Market showed, this was a movement unfussed by issues of decorum. It was happy to mix up the past in any way it saw fit. The obsession with the past was multivalent, never obvious, never just reproduction.

This was particularly clear in the area of housing and architecture, where, as Samuel noted with some irony, the interwar semis and Victorian terraces that had been the subject of decades of opprobrium from political parties, official opinion and cultural history were now being 'reval-ued' as objects of heritage. This rupture in popular taste was in explicit opposition to the modernist project of redevelopment and social transformation through a tech-nologically driven modern architecture:

> In the built environment, the turn against comprehensive clear-ance and high-rise flats, the rise of conservationist sentiment, and the discovery of 'heritage', in what had previously been desig-nated slums, removed at a stroke what had been, ever since the birth of the Labour Party and in the imagination of its Fabian and ILP predecessors, the very essence of the socialist vision: a trans-formation of the built environment, the physical burying of what was conceived of as the nightmare legacy of Victorian industrial-ism and unplanned urban growth. In other countries such matters were secondary to the socialist cause; in Britain they were of its essence.

Meanwhile, the way in which 'history' was now read 'from below' had effects that were not what its largely left-wing (and frequently, like Samuel himself, Communist) advocates could have expected.

> People's history may also have unwittingly prepared the way for more Conservative appropriations of the national past. Its preference for the 'human' document and the close-up view has the effect of domesticating the subject matter of history, and making politics seem irrelevant – so much outside noise. Its very success in rescuing the poor from the 'enormous condescension of posterity' has the unintended effect of rehabilitating the past, opening the nation retrospectively to the excluded. The focus on 'domestic budgeting' and poor people's survival strategies underwrites the values of good housekeeping. The recycling of old photographs – a feature of the 'new' social history – also provides subliminal support for Conservative views of the past. It is difficult to think of the family in terms of oppression and insecurity when photographs testify to its stability and grace.[5]

These phrases, taken from the repertoire of 1980s Thatcherism, resonate with the agenda of the 2010–15 Coalition government and the enforcement of a new, anti-egalitarian austerity. Domestic budgeting, good housekeeping, stability. It sounds as if Samuel is anticipating not only the speeches of David Cameron, but also the televisual world of *Call the Midwife* and *Downton Abbey*, where we are asked to admire a strong, struggling but basically deferent working class that knows its place.

However, Samuel noted that the conservation of the

built environment, and critiques of modern architecture and planning, had not emerged solely from the right. In fact, as when Covent Garden was saved in the 1970s from demolition by self-consciously revolutionary architects at the Greater London Council, this drive to conserve came also from the left, particularly its libertarian strains that emerged after 1968. However, the right capitalised upon it with great speed, replacing the planned landscape of social democracy not with the 'community architecture' of public participation in the inner city, but by letting developers build traditional-looking car-centred cul-de-sacs and retail parks in the outer suburbs. It seems that whenever the left thinks it can turn the past to its own advantage, it is outplayed by the right.

This seems especially to be the case in the many left-wing attempts to present a different version of patriotic and national history. Patrick Wright pointed out this uncomfortable fact during the depths of Thatcherism in his book *On Living in an Old Country*. Here he notes how Thatcher's appeal from very early on annexed the cultural memory of the Second World War to a Conservative narrative of national greatness and assertion. This was then set against the claims of 'wets' who would have us capitulate in the face of the enemy without (the Soviet Union) and the enemy within (the organised working class).

Needless to say, this narrative did not have to be historically accurate in order to be emotionally effective. In 1982, as Wright observes, 'the Second World War [had] been re-declared – not against Hitler, this time, but against the kind of peace that followed it; if Spitfires and Lancasters are in the skies again, they now fly against "socialism" and the "overweening state".[6]

Typically, in response, the left flailed around to produce an adequate counter-narrative, rather 'falling back onto the historical style – the gestures and vocabulary – of a time when solidarity and progress did seem intact, a time when the presence of socialism seemed positive and growing, and when the road did indeed seem to stretch out in front of the marchers'.[7] This was seen, for instance, in 'Tony Benn's resurrectional invocations of the English "people" with their own pre-Marxian drive towards socialism: Peasants' Revolt, Robin Hood and all'. The problem here was that, according to Wright, socialism was inherently future-oriented. Because socialism does not 'present itself as fully achieved or accomplished in the present as we know it, it cannot work up an easy public presence for its sense of history'.

In recent years, some have argued that the real and concrete legacy of the post-war settlement, of social democracy – the council estates, the National Health Service, the comprehensive schools and New Universities, the dribs and drabs left over of social security – are extensive enough that 'the left has something to conserve', as the late historian Tony Judt put it in his influential defence of mainstream (by now almost accidentally 'left') social democracy, *Ill Fares the Land*. With this legacy in mind Judt devoted his last years on earth to arguing for a renewed 'social democracy of fear', able to provide stability in the face of the extreme insecurities of neoliberalism. Somehow, this effort has thus far come to little.

I confess to some feelings of frustration on this count. One of the best arguments for the possibility of a social democracy is the fact that one came damn close to being built between 1945 and 1979, despite its many flaws and omissions. The attacks on social democracy by the 1960s generation that benefitted from it most – as statist, or even 'totalitarian' – now seem hysterical, devoid of any real sense of historical perspective. For them, the 'welfare state' was normal, familiar, and rather boring, a perspective it is hard not to find outright offensive today. Their politics were based on the assumption that affluence, social peace and equality were permanent rather than the brief historical aberration that they were.

Perhaps because of this, I have spent much time as a writer attempting to rehabilitate the built environment created by this moment of social democracy. The fragments of it *do* prove that an egalitarian future is feasible, given that numerous attempts at it still work pretty well in the present day, despite the depredations of Right to Buy, 'decanting', poor maintenance and unemployment. Our grandparents may well have thought a better world than that of laissez-faire capitalism was possible, and had a go at building one, before their children who had been nurtured by it opted instead for a Barratt Home, a 'revalued' Victorian house or a loft conversion in a formerly dark Satanic mill.

Much good work has been done in this vein. A short survey might include John Grindrod's great populist book *Concretopia*; the weblog *Municipal Dreams*; informative and often angry films on post-war social democracy's housing programme, such as Tom Cordell's *Utopia London*, Enrica

Colusso's *Home Sweet Home* on the socially cleansed Heygate Estate, or *Rowley Way Speaks for Itself*, a collectively made film on one of the most successful council estates, Alexandra Road, in North London. There's surely many more I've forgotten. These varied works manage to steer clear of unambiguous nostalgia, through their attention to social history, and the actual voices of architects, residents and their ideas and experiences. However, it seems increasingly doubtful that we can use social democracy's remnants as a stick to beat neoliberal austerity. When it comes to treating the past as a weapon, the Conservative Party are, and always have been, the experts.

So we find ourselves in an increasingly nightmarish situation where an entirely twenty-first-century society – constantly wired up to smartphones and the internet, living via complicated systems of derivatives, credit and unstable property investments, inherently and deeply insecure – appears to console itself with the iconography of a completely different and highly unlike era, to which it is linked solely through liberal use of the 'A' word. So to try and work out how this happened and what can be done about it, this short book will explore the way in which austerity in 2015 dreams of austerity in 1945 and the ways in which it has been used as a weapon and a shibboleth across the political spectrum, in order to ask what might happen at the moment when, finally, we stop keeping calm and carrying on.

1

Lash Out and Cover Up

Advert in pub for pick-me-up tablets — phenacetin or something of the kind.

BLITZ
Thoroughly recommended by the
Medical Profession
The
'LIGHTNING'
Marvellous Discovery
Millions take this remedy
for
Hangover
War Nerves
Influenza
Toothache
Neuralgia
Sleeplessness
Rheumatism
Depression, etc., etc.
Contains no aspirin.

George Orwell, 'War-time Diary',
29 August 1942[1]

The Emblem of Austerity Nostalgia

I can pinpoint the moment when I realised that what had seemed a typically, somewhat insufferably, English phenomenon had gone completely and inescapably global. I was going into the flagship Warsaw branch of the Polish department store Empik and there, just past the revolving doors, was a collection of notebooks, mouse pads, diaries and the like, featuring a familiar English sans serif font, white on red, topped with the crown above the legend, in English:

KEEP CALM

AND

CARRY ON

Aside from the horror film—like feeling that I was being chased wherever I went by an implacable enemy, I was chilled by the proof that this image had finally entered the pantheon of truly global design 'icons'. As an iconic image, it was now there alongside Rosie the Riveter, the muscular female munitions worker on the US World War II propaganda image; as easily identifiable as the headscarved Lily Brik bellowing 'BOOKS!' on Rodchenko's famous poster. As a logo, it was nearly as recognisable as Coca-Cola or Apple. How had this happened? What was it that made the image so popular? How did it manage to grow from a minor English middle-class cult object into an international brand, and what exactly were people saying when they were saying that they were carrying on?

'Keep Calm and Copy', Split, Croatia

My assumption was that the combination of message and design were inextricably tied up with a plethora of English obsessions, from the 'Blitz spirit', through to the cults of the BBC and the NHS and the 1945 post-war consensus. Also contained in this bundle of signifiers was the enduring pretension of an extremely rich (if shoddy and dilapidated) country, the sadomasochistic Toryism imposed by the Conservative–Liberal coalition government of 2010–15, and their presentation of austerity in a manner so brutal and moralistic that it almost seemed to luxuriate in its own parsimony.

Some or none of these thoughts may have been in the heads of the customers at Empik buying their printed tea towels; they may have just thought it was funny. They might have liked it as an example of the slightly dotty retro-Englishness that made them buy those DVDs of *Downton Abbey* with their overdubbed Polski Lektor. However, there are few images of the last decade that are quite so riddled

with ideology, and few 'historical' documents that are quite
so spectacularly false.

It is important to record that the 'Keep Calm and Carry
On' poster was never mass-produced until 2008. It is a historical object of a very peculiar sort. By 2009, when it had
first become hugely popular, it seemed to respond to a particularly English malaise, one connected directly with the
way Britain reacted to the credit crunch and the banking
crash. From this moment of crisis, it tapped into an already
established narrative about Britain's 'finest hour' – the
aerial Battle of Britain in 1940–41 – when it was the only
country left fighting the Third Reich. This was a moment
of entirely indisputable – and apparently uncomplicated –
national heroism, one which Britain has clung to through
thick and thin. Even during the height of the boom, as the
critical theorist Paul Gilroy spotted in his 2004 book *After
Empire*, the Blitz and the Victory were frequently invoked,
made necessary by 'the need to get back to the place or
moment before the country lost its moral and cultural
bearings'.[2] '1940' and '1945' were 'obsessive repetitions',
'anxious and melancholic', morbid fetishes, clung to as a
means of not thinking about other aspects of recent British
history – most obviously, its Empire. This has only intensi-
fied since the financial crisis began.

The 'Blitz spirit' has been exploited by politicians largely
since 1979. When Thatcherites and Blairites spoke of 'hard
choices' and 'muddling through', they often evoked the
memories of 1941. It served to legitimate regimes which
constantly argued that, despite appearances to the contrary,
resources were scarce and there wasn't enough money to

go around; the most persuasive way of explaining why someone (else) was inevitably going to suffer. Ironically, however, this rhetoric of sacrifice was often combined with a demand that the consumers enrich themselves – buy their house, get a new car, make something of themselves, 'aspire'.

Thus, by 2007–08, when the 'end to boom and bust' promised by Gordon Brown appeared to be more than abortive (despite the success of his very 1940s alternative of nationalising the banks and thus 'saving capitalism'), the image appeared for the first time. It's worth noting that shortly after this point, a brief series of protests in 2009–11 were being policed in increasingly ferocious ways. The authorities were allowed to utilise the apparatus of security and surveillance and the proliferation of 'prevention of terrorism' laws set up under the New Labour governments of 1997–2010 to combat any signal of dissent. In this context the poster became ever more ubiquitous, and peculiarly, after 2011, it began to be used in what few protests remained, in an only mildly subverted form.

The 'Keep Calm and Carry On' poster seemed to embody all the contradictions produced by a consumption economy attempting to adapt itself to thrift, and to normalise surveillance and security through an ironic, depoliticised aesthetic. Out of apparent nowhere, this image – combining bare, faintly modernist typography with the consoling logo of the Crown and a similarly reassuring message – spread everywhere.

I first noticed its ubiquity in the winter of 2009, when the poster appeared in dozens of windows in affluent London districts like Blackheath during the prolonged snow and the attendant breakdown of National Rail; the implied message about hardiness in the face of adversity and the Blitz spirit looked rather absurd in the context of a dusting of snow crippling the railway system. The poster seemed to exemplify a design phenomenon that had slowly crept up on us in the last few years to the point where it became unavoidable. It's best described as *Austerity Nostalgia*. This aesthetic took the form of a nostalgia for the kind of public modernism that, rightly or wrongly, was seen to have characterised the period from the 1930s to the early 70s; it could just as easily exemplify a more straightforwardly conservative longing for security and stability in the face of hard times. Above all, though, the poster was the most visible form of a vague nostalgia for a benevolent, quasi-modernist English bureaucratic aesthetic.

Yet its spread, and its political adaptations, managed to create a sort of ironic visual authoritarianism, in direct correlation with an entirely un-ironic intensification of repression and police violence. After the unrest of 2011 fizzled out, the poster seemed to become a self-satisfying declaration of the refusal to resist austerity, and instead offer a commitment to plod glumly on in an increasingly intolerable situation. However, its main affect was not about the present as such, but about a remarkably distorted idea of the past.

Unlike many forms of nostalgia, the memory invoked by the 'Keep Calm and Carry On' poster is not based on lived experience. Most of those who have bought this poster, or worn the various bags, T-shirts and other memorabilia based upon it, were probably born in the 1970s or 80s. They have no memory whatsoever of the kind of benevolent statism the slogan purports to exemplify. In that sense, the poster is an example of the phenomenon given a capsule definition by Douglas Coupland in 1991: 'Legislated Nostalgia', that is, 'to force a body of people to have memories they do not actually possess'.[3]

However, there's more to it than that. Even someone who was around at the time, unless they'd worked at the department of the Ministry of Information that actually designed the poster, would never have seen it. In fact, before 2008, few had ever encountered 'Keep Calm and Carry On' displayed in a public place.

It was designed for the Ministry of Information in 1939, but the poster's 'official website', which sells a variety of Keep-Calm-and-Carry-On tat,[4] mentions that it never became an official propaganda poster. Rather, only a handful had been printed on a test basis. The specific purpose of the poster was to 'stiffen resolve' in the event of a Nazi invasion, and it was one in a set of three. There were two others in the series, which followed the exact same design principles – a slogan in a sans serif font with resemblances to (but not, in fact) Gill Sans, centred on a block-colour background, with the crown above. The others were:

YOUR COURAGE
YOUR CHEERFULNESS
YOUR RESOLUTION
WILL BRING
US VICTORY

And:

FREEDOM IS
IN PERIL
DEFEND IT
WITH ALL
YOUR MIGHT

Both of these were printed up, and 'YOUR COURAGE …' was particularly widely displayed during the Blitz, given that the feared invasion did not take place after the German defeat in the Battle of Britain. You can see one on a billboard in the background of the last scene of Michael Powell and Emeric Pressburger's 1943 film, *The Life and Death of Colonel Blimp*, when the ageing, reactionary but charming soldier finds his house in Belgravia bombed.

Of the three proposals, 'KEEP CALM AND CARRY ON' was, for some reason, discarded after the test printing, and it never found its way to public display. Possibly, this was because it was considered less appropriate to the conditions of the Blitz than to the mass panic expected in the event of a German ground invasion. One of those few test printings of the poster was found in amongst a consignment of second-hand books bought at auction by Barter Books in Alnwick, Northumberland, who then produced the first reproductions.

Initially sold in London by the shop at the Victoria and Albert Museum, it became a middlebrow staple when the recession, initially merely the slightly euphemistic 'credit crunch', hit. Through this poster, the way to display one's commitment to the new austerity regime was to buy more consumer goods, albeit with a less garish aesthetic than was customary during the boom. This was no different to the 'keep calm and carry on shopping' commanded by George W. Bush both after September 11 and when the sub-prime crisis hit America. The 'wartime' use of this rhetoric escalated during the economic turmoil in the UK; witness the slogans of the 2010–15 coalition government, from 'We're All in This Together' to 'We've maxed out our credit card'.

The power of 'Keep Calm and Carry On' comes from a yearning for an actual or imaginary English patrician attitude of stiff upper lips and muddling through. This is, however, something that largely survives only in the popular imaginary, in a country devoted to services and consumption, and where elections are decided on the basis of house price value, and given to sudden, mawkish outpourings of sentiment. The poster isn't just a case of the return of the repressed, it is rather the return of repression itself. It is *a nostalgia for the state of being repressed* – solid, stoic, public-spirited, as opposed to the depoliticised, hysterical and privatised reality of Britain over the last thirty years.

At the same time as it evokes a sense of loss over the decline of an idea of Britain and the British, it is both reassuring and flattering, implying a virtuous (if highly self-aware) consumer stoicism. Of course, in the end, it's a bit of a joke: you don't really think your pay cut or your children's inability to buy a house, or the fact that someone somewhere else has been made homeless because of the bedroom tax, or lost their benefit, or worked on a zero-hours contract, is really comparable to the Blitz – but it's all a bit of fun, isn't it?

Austere Consumerism

The 'Keep Calm and Carry On' poster is only the tip of an iceberg of austerity nostalgia. Although early examples of the mood can be seen as a reaction to the 'threat of terrorism' and the allegedly attendant 'Blitz spirit', it has become an increasingly prevalent response to the uncertainties of economic collapse.

One of the first places this happened was in food, an area closely connected with the immediate satisfaction of desires. Along with the Blitz came rationing, which was of course not fully abolished until the mid-1950s. Accounts of this vary; its egalitarianism meant that while the middle classes experienced a drastic decline in the quality and quantity of their diet, for many of the poor it was a minor improvement.

Either way, it was a grim regime, aided by the emergence of various by-products and substitutes – Spam, corned beef – which stuck around in the already famously dismal British diet for some time to come, before mass immigration gradually made eating in Britain less awful. In the process, entire aspects of British cuisine – the sort of thing listed by George Orwell in his essay 'In Praise of English Cooking', such as suet dumplings, Lancashire hotpot, Yorkshire pudding, roast dinners, faggots, spotted dick, toad in the hole – began to disappear, at least from the metropoles.

The figure of importance here is the Essex multimillionaire chef and Winston Churchill fan Jamie Oliver. Clearly as decent and sincere a person as you'll find on the *Sunday Times* Rich List, his various crusades for good food and the manner in which he markets them are inadvertently very telling. After his initial fame as a New Labour–era star, a relatively young and Beckham-coiffed celebrity chef, his main concern (aside from a massive high-end chain restaurant empire that stretches from Greenwich Market to the Hotel Moskva) has been to take 'good food' – locally sourced, cooked from scratch – from being a preserve of the middle classes and bringing it to the 'disadvantaged' and 'socially excluded' of inner-city London, ex-industrial towns, mining villages and other places slashed and burned by thirty-plus years of Thatcherism.

The first version of this was the TV series *Jamie's School Dinners*, where a camera crew documented him trying to influence the school meals choices of a comprehensive in Kidbrooke, a poor, and recently almost totally demolished, area in South-East London. Notoriously, this crusade was nearly thwarted by mothers bringing their kids fizzy drinks and burgers that they pushed through the fences, so that their kids wouldn't have to suffer that healthy-eating muck.

The second phase was the book, TV series and chain of shops branded as *The Ministry of Food*. The name is taken directly from the actual wartime ministry charged with managing the rationed food economy of war-torn Britain. Using the assistance of a few public bodies, setting up a charity, pouring in some coalfield regeneration money and some money of his own, he planned to teach the proletariat to make itself real food with real ingredients. One could argue that he was the latest in a long line of middle-class people lecturing the lower orders on their choice of nutrition, part of an immense construction of grotesque neo-Victorian snobbery – *How Clean Is Your House*, *Benefits Street*, *Immigration Street*, exercises in *Let's laugh at Picturesque Prole Scum* – but Oliver got in there, and 'got his hands dirty'.

However, the story ended in a predictable manner: attempts to build this charitable action into something permanent and institutional foundered on the disinclination of any plausible British government to antagonise the supermarkets and sundry manufacturers who funnel money to both the two main political parties. The appeal to a time when things like food or information were apparently dispensed by a benign paternalist bureaucracy, before consumer choice carried all before it, can only be translated into the infrastructure of charity and PR, where we learn what happens over a few months during a TV show and then forget about it. A 'permanent' network of Ministry of Food shops, 'pop-ups' which taught cooking skills and had a mostly voluntary staff, were set up in the north of England in Bradford, Leeds, Newcastle, and Rotherham, though this last was forced to close following health and safety concerns in 2013.[5]

Much more influential than this up-by-your-bootstraps attempt to do a TV/charity version of the welfare state was the Ministry's aesthetics. On the cover of the tie-in cookbook, Oliver sits up to a table laid with a 1940s 'utility' tablecloth in front of some bleakly cute post-war wallpaper, and MINISTRY OF FOOD is declared in that same derivative of Gill Sans as the Keep Calm poster.

This is familiar territory. There's a whole micro-industry of austerity nostalgia aimed straight at the stomach. Of course there's Oliver's own chain of 'Jamie's' restaurants, where you can order pork scratchings for £4 (they come with a side of English mustard) and enjoy neo-Victorian toilets. Beyond Jamie's empire, middle-class operations such as caterers Peyton and Byrne combine the sort of retro food common across the Western world (lots of cupcakes) with elaborate versions of simple English grub like sausage and mash. Some of the interiors of their cafes (such as the one in Heals, Tottenham Court Road) have been designed by architects FAT in a pop spin on the faintly lavatorial, institutional design common to the surviving fragments of genuine 1940s Britain that can still be found scattered around the UK – pie and mash shops in Deptford, ice

Austerity Grub, Albion, NeoBankside

cream parlours in Worthing, the dingier Glasgow pubs, all featuring lots of wipe-clean tiles.

Other versions of this are more luxurious, such as Dinner, where Heston Blumenthal provides 'typically quirky' English food as part of the attractions of One Hyde Park, the most expensive housing development on earth. Something similar is offered at Canteen, which has branches in the Royal Festival Hall, Canary Wharf, and – after its scorched-earth gentrification courtesy of the Corporation of London and Norman Foster – Spitalfields Market. Canteen serves 'Great British Food', where the 'beers, ciders and perrys represent our country's brewing history' and even the cocktails are 'British-led'.[6] The interior design is clearly part of the appeal, offering a strange, luxurious version of a works canteen, with benches, trays and sans serif signs that aim to be both modernist and nostalgic. It presents the incongruous spectacle of the very comfortable booking themselves into the dining hall of a branch of Tyrell and Green circa 1960.

Still more bizarre is Albion, a greengrocer for oligarchs, selling traditional English produce to the denizens of NEO Bankside, the Richard Rogers–designed towers alongside the Tate Modern. Built into the ground floor of one of the towers, it sells its unpretentious fruit and veg next to posters advertising flats that start at the knock-down price of £2 million.

The link between British food and austerity nostalgia is in many ways pretty apt. The stodge of pie pastry, sausage meat, and especially that seemingly forgotten by-product suet is instantly reassuring, familiar, old-fashioned; like food in general, it is experienced in an intimate, barely conscious way. For those of us in our thirties, it's not a connection with the food of our parents – the generation of the 1970s and 80s preferred Findus and boil-in-the-bag (working class), or Elizabeth David/Marks and Sparks cookbook fare (middle class), and fed us the same stuff. No, it's our grandparents' food, sweet and stodgy and reminiscent of a bygone era. Meanwhile, plenty of 'real' austerity consumerism exists, and you can find it in any supermarket: there is little more austere than Tesco Value (with those stripes, it's almost like actual 1940s utility design) or Sainsbury's Basics (with its cute little slogans telling you that the 10p soap has fewer bubbles, but still lathers you up a treat). It's also the lowest-quality stuff available, the basest by-products of industrialised food production, precisely the sort of thing that Jamie Oliver wants to save our kids and our northerners from.

While most of this is the aesthetic and culinary equivalent of a wealthy person collecting money-off vouchers, closer to the reality as lived by most people is a mobile app called the Ration Book. On its website, the Ration Book gives you a crash course on rationing, when the government made sure that in the face of shortage and blockade the population could still get 'life's essentials' in the form of the famous book, with its stamps to get X amount of dried egg, flour, pollock and Spam. It is an app that aggregates discounts on various brands via voucher codes for those facing the 'crunch' – the people the unfortunate Ed Miliband tried to reach out to as the 'squeezed middle'. 'Our team of "Ministers" broker the best deals with the biggest

brands, to give you the best value'.[7] Is there any better way
of describing the UK in the second decade of the twenty-
first century than as the sort of country that produces apps
to simulate state rationing of basic goods, simply to shave a
little bit off the price of 'high street brands'?

This sort of austerity nostalgia of the stomach is one way
in which folk's peculiar longing for the 1940s is conveyed;
much more can be found in music and design. Walk into the
shop at the Royal Festival Hall or the Imperial War Museum
in London, and you'll find an avalanche of it. Posters from
the 1940s, toys and trinkets, none of them later than circa
1965, have been resurrected from the dustbin of history and
laid out for you to buy, along with austerity cookbooks, the
Design series of books on pre-1960s 'iconic' graphic artists
like Abram Games, David Gentleman, Eric Ravilious, et
al., plus a whole cornucopia of Keep Calm–related accou-
trements. A particularly established example is the use of
the 1930s Penguin book covers as an 'iconic' logo for all

The Emporium of Austerity Nostalgia, Royal Festival Hall, London

The Trellick Tower mug

manner of goods, deliberately calling to mind Penguin's mid-century role as a substantially educative publisher.

Then there are all those prints of modernist buildings, ready for you to frame and place in your ex-council flat in Zone 2 or 3: reduced, stark blow-ups of the outlines of modernist architecture, whether demolished (the 'Get Carter' Trinity Square car park in Gateshead) or protected (London's National Theatre). The plate-making company People Will Always Need Plates have made a name for themselves with towels, mugs, plates and badges emblazoned with various British modernist buildings from the 1930s to the 1960s, elegantly redrawn in a bold, schematic form that sidesteps the often rather shabby reality of the buildings.

However, by recreating the pure image of the historically untainted building, they manage to precisely reverse the original modernist ethos. If for Adolf Loos and generations of modernist architects ornament was crime, here modernist buildings are made into ornaments. Still, the choice of buildings is politically interesting. Blocks of 1930s collective housing, 1960s council flats, interwar London Underground stations – exactly the sort of architectural programmes now considered obsolete in favour of retail and property speculation.

Some of the buildings immortalised in these plates have been the subject of direct transfers of assets from the public sector into the private. The reclamation of post-war modernist architecture by the intelligentsia has been a contributory factor in the privatisation of social housing. An early instance of this was the sell-off of Keeling House, Denys Lasdun's East London 'Cluster Block', to a private developer, who promptly marketed the flats to 'creatives'. A series of gentrifications of modernist social housing followed, from the Brunswick Centre in Bloomsbury (turned from a rotting brutalist megastructure into the home of London's largest branch of Waitrose), to Park Hill, an architecturally extraordinary council estate in Sheffield, given away for free to the Mancunian developer Urban Splash, whose own favouring of 'compact' flats has long been an example of austerity sold as luxury – although after the boom, their privatisation scheme had to be bailed out by millions of pounds in public money.

A less obviously complicit example of this is the modifications of post-war design into something more eerie and psychedelic practised by the Ghost Box record label. For their first few years, each cover was modelled closely on Germano Facetti's book covers for Pelican, Penguin's educational arm (recently resurrected with appropriately retro designs). Ghost Box play with the notion of an enlightened, aesthetically advanced bureaucracy, through references to the functionalist *musique concrète* of the BBC Radiophonic Workshop and the authoritative Received Pronunciation voices of reconstructed, re-enacted or fictional public service broadcasts, referencing both road safety films and the apocalyptic horror of the 1970s *Protect and Survive* films that were designed to be broadcast in the event of a likely imminence of nuclear war. The names of the groups were a more recondite version of the Ministry of Food in their evocation of a bygone public bureaucracy, lofty and patrician, slightly sinister: the Advisory Circle, Belbury Poly, the Focus Group, all coming to prominence around 2007, at the same time as the Keep Calm poster. At their best – say, the blurred, gap-filled, gimcrack constructions of the Focus Group's *Hey Let Loose Your Love* (2005) – Ghost Box records could be a rare example of austerity nostalgia as something genuinely unnerving. The fog and mess of actual memory, and a persistent hint of the uncanny, prevents them from being merely reassuring.

In this they are perhaps an exception to the prevalent trend. Their aesthetic was described by Mark Fisher, borrowing a phrase from Jacques Derrida's *Spectres of Marx*, as 'hauntological' – a sort of return of the social democratic repressed, but a return as a rupture; an aesthetic warped by the intervention of forgetting, vague recollection, and fifty years of history, creating instead of 'heritage' a dream-world of public modernism which never fully existed, running together moments that didn't coincide. 'What if rock and roll didn't happen, and jazz continued on a strange trajectory. I had this other image of a mass hysteria at the Festival of Britain', as the label's Julian House fantasised.[8]

Instead of hankering for the past in the context of neoliberalism's unforgiving bull market, the Ghost Box aesthetic suggests a haunting of the present by the unfulfilled promises of the past.[9] But this style too, with its curatorial assemblage of refracted references to public information films, electronic TV cues, nuclear anxiety and modernist public improvement, soon became as reassuring and bourgeois as a hearty plate of Peyton and Byrne sausage and mash.[10] The reference points were so easily learned – British horror films plus modernist book design plus modernist architecture plus pre-1979 public TV plus un-pop electronic music – that they became easily replicated, another microgenre to be a fixture on the more recondite music festival circuit.

Entire films, like *Berberian Sound Studio*, or festivals, such as Unsound in Krakow, when the Polish historic capital becomes part of Hackney for a week, are 'hauntological'; a group even appeared in 2014 called the Hauntologists. Remarkably, something as odd as the longing for the material world of social democracy became an identifiable and marketable musical genre, with a section in the more recherché London or Glasgow record shops. In a critique in the Northampton-based publication *Dodgem Logic*, Gary Mills, formerly one half of the 'hauntological' group Mordant Music, subjected the entire experiment to a convincing critique, arguing that all this clever conceptual play ultimately becomes a 'reverential whimsy', which 'offers more of the same: the 1960s. Revivalism.'[11]

Mordant Music's DVD *MisinforMation* can be seen as a way of salvaging something of interest from this entire farrago. Allowed to ransack the public information films of the Central Office of Information, the group's mission was to disturb rather than reassure, creating an increasingly nightmarish, repetitious montage of demotic English grimness, Cold War terror and sudden images of utopian possibility, always brutally snatched away as the viewer/listener is plunged right back into a mess of meaningless slogans and shocking images of fire, injury and disaster. Similarly, their 2009 album *SyMptoMs* was unusually bitter and angry about this 'hauntological' condition, sounding like music made by middle-aged synthesiser-owning men forced to work the rest of their lives in the Luton Arndale Centre.

Ultimately, however, like all pop trends, hauntology gradually became mainstream, although in a way that the likes of Julian House couldn't have imagined – the nostalgia for non-pop, pre-1979 modern Britain assimilated into just another part of a hard right-wing neoliberalism which, in England at least, seems impregnable, financial crisis or no financial crisis.

Ironic Authoritarianism

The first myth of 'Keep Calm and Carry On' is that of the benevolent state. This myth adopts the same austerity aesthetic as the popular poster to disguise its iron determination.

Take, for example, the manufactured nostalgia for the watchful, protective eye of public institutions. Perhaps

the earliest example was provided by the poster designers of Transport for London, the beleaguered, publicly
owned transport network created by Ken Livingstone as
Mayor of London in 2000. TfL began by trying to reverse
privatisation and ended up embracing it, in the form of
the PFI-funded East London Line extension. From 2002,
a series of posters appeared on bus shelters with slogans
such as 'Secure Beneath the Watchful Eyes', with said eyes
depicted as CCTV cameras. These images had distinct similarities in their typography with 1930s posters for London
Transport by the Bauhaus designer László Moholy-Nagy.
They quite deliberately played with the Orwellian associations of 1930s and 40s design, the benign eyes watching
over London's busy commuters explicitly styled in mock-
totalitarian terms.

This is, however, a rather queasy joke. London has some
of the heaviest surveillance in the world, and more CCTV
cameras than any other city. To treat this as cheery benevo-
lence is deeply dubious. The poster advertises the allegedly
caring role of the Metropolitan Police in their surveillance
of the bus or Tube passenger, something that could only
leave a nasty taste in the mouth after the death of Jean-
Charles de Menezes, shot by the Met in July 2006 in the
days following the 7/7 bombings.

The great irony of all this is that the supposedly overbear-
ing, paternalistic public institutions of the 1940s were either
unable or unwilling to set up the apparatus of surveillance
that every Londoner now regards as normal. What Orwell
hadn't realised was that the surveillance society would be
accompanied by ironic jokes, not shrill exhortations.

In April 2009, another series of posters appeared on British streets, this time on behalf of the police. Based ostentatiously on 'Keep Calm', they share the same centred design and humanist sans serifs, only replacing the crown with the police badge. The text consists of three slogans, inspired by particular clichés used by the police in the popular imagination, albeit in one case with a decidedly sinister twist;

WE'D LIKE
TO GIVE
YOU
A GOOD
TALKING TO;

ANYTHING
YOU SAY
MAY
BE TAKEN DOWN
AND USED AS
EVIDENCE;

and, remarkably,

YOU HAVE THE RIGHT
<u>NOT</u>
TO REMAIN SILENT.

Underneath, in extremely small, easily missed print, is the official message based on the Policing Pledge, one of the many managerial initiatives intended to 'restore confidence' or 'enable choice' in one or another public body. For instance, the 'talking to' poster pledges to listen to the consumer of policing, while the '<u>not</u> to remain silent' poster encourages you to make a complaint against the police should they inconvenience you. In the twist between an authoritarian exclamation and the liberal, caring small print that, supposedly, gives an amusing gloss to the large print, these are spectacular examples of disavowal and the use of irony to say appalling things unchallenged.

The sleight of hand is deft. The pay-off appears in small print, reminding us that really the police force are all about helping old ladies across the road: 'the police now pledge to listen …' The truth, of course, is in large print. Given the suspension of habeas corpus for suspected 'terrorists', you genuinely do not have the right to remain silent. So, while this 'witty' gesture claims to play with the brutally state-protecting image of the police, it also declares, very loudly, that the rules no longer apply.

Keep Calm and Pay Back

The true obscenity of these police posters was made obvious in an advertisement produced by the Ministry of Justice, which ran in local papers in spring 2009; the version I have is pulled from the South London *Mercury* on 1 April. Again, the centring of a vaguely Eric Gill-esque typography, again the large message and small print, again the replacement of the crown, this time by the coat of arms of the Ministry of Justice. The background this time isn't the original red, or the police posters' blue, but a Guantánamo orange. The slogan this time:

HAVE YOUR SAY
ON HOW
CRIMINALS
PAY BACK

This was a reference to the Community Payback scheme, an intensification of community service, where petty criminals are made to work in ostentatiously bright outfits, in gangs, as a display of their debt to the public – 'Justice Seen, Justice Done', as another Ministry of Justice slogan at the foot of the poster has it.

The advertisement explains:

Community Payback is a punishment that can be handed out by the courts. It's physical work, carried out by criminals in the community. Offenders have to wear bright orange jackets marked Community Payback, so you'll see them paying back for their crimes. Members of the public can have their say on where offenders are working and the kind of work they are doing.

To witness an instance of Community Payback, as I did in 2009 on a Greenwich council estate, is an alarming experience – a score of downcast black youth, being led by a similarly orange-jacketed overseer to pick up rubbish in an area where the council infrequently collected. The Community, meanwhile, on this weekday morning, were conspicuous by their absence, so that this was a display without an audience. Yet it is a spectacular method of punishment intended to be watched and, it would seem, enjoyed. The description in the ad's small print epitomises one of the most salient features of Blairite discipline: the tabloid-courting methods of punishment, inching as close as possible to public humiliation while stopping short of outright violence. This combines with the focus-group/ *Guardian*-supplement usage of 'community' to mean something cosy and shared. Meanwhile the macho use of 'payback' offers a final authoritarian stamp. Note, too, that this is all about 'choice' and 'empowerment', in that the Community is asked to specifically choose the punishment for the petty criminal. The ad offers few clues as to what this might entail, but the message is more important than the actual possibility that the victim of a burglary might ask orange-jacketed teenagers to weed their front gardens.

Here the dividing line between authoritarianism as design in-joke and as actual political practice has definitively been erased.

Yet what made these posters and advertisements especially remarkable was that they coincided with one of the first eruptions of public discontent after the financial crisis –

the G20 protests on 1 April, in the City of London. In the preceding months, the police had promised violence, to the extent of issuing a statement of unusual aggression declaring themselves to be 'up for it'. Meanwhile, new anti-terrorism laws made photographing policemen potentially illegal, if it could be proven that they were in the midst of an approximately anti-terrorist activity, or if the photographs could be useful for terrorists themselves.

Within minutes of entering the space between the Bank of England and the Royal Exchange, it was obvious that the police were intent on a riot, irrespective of what the protesters wanted. The 'kettle' in which the G20 protesters were enclosed became the site, later recorded on digital cameras and mobile phones, of women being hit for talking back, of climate camp protesters with their hands in the air being baton-charged, of police medics wielding truncheons, and, most famously, of the manslaughter (at least) of a passer-by, Ian Tomlinson.

In the aftermath of the police riot and the blizzard of false information on Tomlinson's death, an anonymous internet user produced a variant on the 'Keep Calm' poster, sadly photoshopped into a bus-stop billboard rather than replacing one of the actual posters: 'Lash Out and Cover Up'. This act of *détournement* seemed decidedly appropriate, if impotent. It applied all the more the following year, when the unexpectedly massive student protests were quickly crushed by kettling and, when necessary, the cracking of heads.

The same shrillness can be seen in the adaptation of the poster by Britain's privatised energy companies, when they were threatened with minor price caps in one of those wildly Bolshevik policies of 'Red Ed' Miliband. A poster I've seen on numerous occasions in corner shops reads:

PAY BILLS

AND

CARRY ON

Here, the crown is absent, but instead, little white icons on the red background show the various things you can pay bills for — a flame, a light bulb, a house, a tap. This is an advert for PayPoint, the company whose machines enable you to pay bills in cash in corner shops, if your income is too unreliable for a regular standing order or direct debit.

There is something particularly sick and sarcastic in this assimilation of the iconography of the era of British Rail to the purposes of such ruthless vultures on the public sector as E.ON, Thames Water and the like. You could now feel

Keep Calm and Pay Bills

like you were performing an act of Blitz Spirit virtuousness as you paid some extortionate sum of money to a private company that is, in many cases, owned by a public company in France or a pension fund in Canada.

Then, as 'Keep Calm' and its permutations continued to evolve, the poster started being seen in what protests there were after the first, surprisingly lively response to the Coalition's assault on the debris of the welfare state – the student protests of winter 2010–11, or the huge TUC demonstration of March 2011. In the aftermath of the riots of August 2011 it was prominently on display during the broom-wielding 'clean-up' that took place in the more (or partly) affluent areas affected. Here young people got dressed up, often in some version of 1940s costume, to exhibit their disgust with the way that other, poorer young people had, in the course of the riot, stolen vulgar things like twenty-first-century sportswear.

After that, the Save Lewisham Hospital campaign of 2012 was one of the more successful examples of resistance. Although it was difficult for anyone other than the cowed trade unions or a barely awake Labour Party to stop the 2010 Health and Social Care bill that effectively privatised the NHS, certain side effects of it could be, and were, questioned. When the large South-East London General Hospital was threatened with the closure of its Accident and Emergency and Maternity departments, large demonstrations ensued, with tens of thousands marching through the streets of Lewisham. The campaign also produced placards and posters based on Keep Calm and Carry On. Typical was

DON'T KEEP CALM
GET ANGRY
AND SAVE
LEWISHAM A & E

on the usual red background, with the crown still at the top, displayed in hundreds of windows across South-East London.

In the end, the protests were successful in terms of their immediate objectives, although the hospital is still being sliced up and handed over in morsels to private service corporations like Serco.

This was a political variant on the countless Keep Calm parodies that emerged in frustration at the poster's smugness – 'Flip Out and Get Angry', and so forth. Now, it's quite possible that the conformism of this imagery – its appeal to the crown, the familiarity of the image, the stark yet reassuring layout of the poster, its extreme design clarity (unencumbered by the usual sub-constructivist old-punk crap typical of the Socialist Worker placards that once swamped every demonstration) means that the problem and the slogan are instantly conveyed to anyone going past the poster on the bus. However, the use or 'subversion' of the poster is the symptom of something wider – the attempt to create a left-wing version of austerity nostalgia, one that could close the massive gap between Austerity 1945 and Austerity 2015.

2

Can the Ghost of Clement Attlee Save Us?

We hired a rowing boat and rowed out into the Sea of Galilee ...
Coming in, we entered a little Arab restaurant for refreshment and as we
walked towards the place, a Jew hurried up with a smile and said 'The
war — finished!' ...

Then the national dances began — Germans, Czechs, Poles, Turks,
Yugoslavs, all did their national dances. Then there was a pause and an
announcement in Hebrew. Everyone looked at us and it was explained
that the RAF officers would do an English national dance. Hurriedly
deciding to do the boomps-a-daisy, two of us took the floor — it was an
instantaneous success and everybody joined in.

RAF pilot Tony Benn, stationed in Palestine,
diary entry for VE Day, 7 May 1945[1]

The Save Lewisham Hospital campaign was not the only example of the attempt by left-wing causes to try and produce their own version of austerity nostalgia and turn it to political ends.

Recall Danny Boyle's opening ceremony for the Olympic Games held in London in 2012. Boyle's pageant invoked the legacies of the British documentary movement of the 1930s and 40s, with a depiction of the industrial revolution explicitly indebted to filmmaker Humphrey Jennings's book *Pandaemonium*. The war gives way to the construction of the welfare state, and especially the National Health Service, whose emergence becomes the centrepiece of the whole performance. Compared to the imperial pageantry expected at such occasions, it was taken as a vivid and timely reminder of the radical institutions that the Coalition government were, at that point, busy dismantling.

Nonetheless, austerity nostalgia is in large degree a right-wing phenomenon. The background noise of television programmes like *Downton Abbey* and *Call the Midwife* promote a 1940s and 50s where the working class was diligent and deferent, rather than prone to strikes and keen to embrace a new modernist world, whether that of the new estates and new towns or that of pop music and fashion.

However odd this might seem, given that 1945 has long been interpreted as the high-water mark of English socialism, the appeal to the 1940s begins on the Labour right, rather than the left. Or rather, a peculiar combination of the Tory left and the Labour right, working in tandem.[2]

Arguably the earliest examples of austerity nostalgia in recent politics was the report *The New East End*, by Geoff Dench, Kate Gavron and Michael Young, presented as a direct successor to Peter Wilmot and Michael Young's famous post-war study, *Family and Kinship in East London*. *The New East End* was written by fellows at the Young Foundation, a think tank with close links to the Labour Party. It was hailed for its sceptical analysis of 'multiculturalism' and for its exploration of the collective psyche of the so-called white working class, a group described by one of its advocates, the journalist Michael Collins, as a 'forgotten tribe'.

The study blamed Muslims of East London for not 'integrating' and for indulging in Tammany Hall or 'communalist' politics. It also focused on the way that the 'indigenous' East Enders were being pushed out (presumably by the poorer incomers, certainly not by the yuppie influx into Canary Wharf or Wapping, or the move of young hipsters into Bethnal Green and Hackney) yet remained obsessed with the war and the Blitz, distant experiences that still shaped their consciousness. Their sense of having created the welfare state was, according to the authors, mixed with a belief that it was now being exploited by Muslims, single mums, immigrants, whoever.

Rather than challenging this empirically false belief, the response in much of the British left was to pander to it. The theoretical matrix for this, meanwhile, was laid down by a professed conservative, the think tanker Phillip Blond, whose self-description in 2010 as a 'Red Tory' included the defence of a welfare state ensuring a deferent, stable, traditional nuclear family, alongside a distrust of the descendants of Britain's imperial subjects, who made the mistake of thinking that the welfare state existed for them, too.[2]

This combination was neatly reversed into 'Blue Labour' by the centrist Labour MP and Portsmouth native Jon Cruddas and the social democratic scholar Maurice Glasman, both of whom were smart enough to know better. At the same time, some new aspects were pulled into the equation that the wonks of *The New East End* and *Red Tory* wouldn't have noticed. For Cruddas and Glasman, the intellectual forbears of this tradition were George Orwell – who told us in the 1940s that those whose heart had not leapt at the sight of the Union Jack would shrink from revolution – and a more left-field figure, the historian E. P. Thompson, whose *Making of the English Working Class* (1963) is a work of Marxist history that stresses the deep roots of English radical politics. Cruddas, for instance, picked up the demand for an English Parliament from odd right-wing groups like the English Democrats, and gave it a left spin – such a parliament, he asserted, would be based in York, and 'Jerusalem' would be its anthem.

These same debates were beginning to filter into popular culture. One influential book of the period was a memoir by the long-standing Labour supporter and early adopter of austerity chic in the 1980s, Billy Bragg, entitled *The Progressive Patriot*. Bragg did not flirt with racism in the way that many of these writers have done; the 'patriotism' that he refers to was that of tolerance and multiculturalism. The intended effect was to make radicalism a specifically English virtue.

The wager is that we can, just by tapping into our own history, find a real popular radicalism that resonates with ordinary people, rather than with small groups of intellectuals discussing Fully Automated Luxury Communism.

All these notions had a major role in Labour's policy-making under Ed Miliband. Though the son of a Belgian-Polish-Jewish migrant who spent his life arguing that English nationalism could not save Labour, the younger

Miliband made a strong attempt to do just that. Austerity was not to be renounced, of course, Labour wonks having noticed its strange popularity with much of the middle class; but it was not the middle class who were invoked as justification.

Instead Labour aimed to inspire a mildly leftist populism in order to bend the economy towards the interests of 'producers' rather than 'predators', with notionally redistributive policies like rent controls, strictures on (though no renationalisation of) energy companies, and partial renationalisation of the NHS via repealing the Health and Social Care Act. These would be combined with appeals against immigration, immortalised in an infamous Labour Party 'Controls on Immigration' mug, and stout positions on defence and maintaining Britain's position in the world.

Needless to say, this version of austerity-nostalgia politics, devised to a very large degree by Cruddas, proved deeply unsuccessful in winning back the millions of working- and lower-middle-class voters who had deserted Labour under Tony Blair. But the argument that the left is most successful when it can align with some kind of patriotism was seen to be vindicated by the enormous success of the Scottish Nationalist Party, especially after it narrowly lost the 2014 referendum on independence and swept Scotland in the 2015 General Election.

1945 remains the English left's eternal benchmark, the moment when war led to its greatest parliamentary triumph. That this combination is utterly unrepeatable is seldom considered. But in theory the left is impelled to a more inclusive, more humane version of 'socialism and the

English genius', to use Orwell's phrase. This, then, is the 'social democracy of fear' as a politics, one which tries to annex ground from the right without partaking in any of the 'sad passions' that actually makes much of the right's politics so powerful – resentment, hatred, bitterness.

The problem in any possible switch from 'regressive' to 'progressive' patriotism is context, and the fact that most English nationalists do not see themselves as left-wingers who have not been appealed to properly. In 1945, however tenuous and hypocritical it was, socialism and English identity became linked in a moment of real existential danger, through the exceptional circumstances of total mobilisation and wartime nationalisation, which enforced both equality and patriotism. In Scotland today, the election results and opinion polls made clear that most Yes voters were motivated by a desire to escape England's political dominance – in other words, its inflicting of Tory governments – and were concentrated not in the traditionalist shires, but in Glasgow, Scotland's biggest, most multiracial city. The appeal to 'patriotism' was interpreted by Yes voters – rightly or wrongly – as a call to social democracy.

What, though, if the left could ignore nationalism but appeal to the 1940s and the 'post-war consensus' without pandering to racism and division?

Land of Broken Promise

Three popular, well-received documentary films in particular give a sense of the way that austerity nostalgia could be utilised.

One of them is by a major director of feature films – Ken Loach's *The Spirit of '45* (2013); one is a young documentary maker's exploration of the late Tony Benn's *Will and Testament* (2014); and another comes from the avant-garde, Luke Fowler's exploration of E. P. Thompson in *The Poor Stockinger, the Luddite Cropper and the Deluded Followers of Joanna Southcott* (2012). In their different ways, all lay claim to the legacies of the welfare state, and try to will them back into being, or at best, remind people of their existence and their possibility.

The Spirit of '45 is a rare documentary from Loach, the veteran British socialist-realist filmmaker. His first was *What Side Are You On?*, about the miners' support groups of the mid-1980s. Like that film, *The Spirit of '45* appears to have been an intervention, an urgent commentary on something about which the director feels particularly strongly, specifically, the dismantlement of the welfare state by the Coalition government.

The film begins with swing music and people – mainly women – celebrating VE day, as written accounts of the event are read out over footage detailing the (frankly lusty) celebrations on Trafalgar Square. The working-class, female voices remind us of what they've just emerged from. Then the screen moves to the 'present', shot in the same bled-out grey as the historic footage. A Geordie voice asks: 'Will we defeat our pre-war enemies?' 'Everything was run by rich people, for rich people', says a GP, today. 'It was them and us', repeats a miner. The quick-fire film footage that runs between these new, living, if elderly voices, is interspersed with a ragbag taken from newsreels, amateur footage and, most of all, the short films of the British documentary movement of the interwar years, all bleached to the same grey so that there is no jaggedness or contrast between images of now and then.

The accounts of poverty accumulate in rapid succession. Liverpudlian Sam Watts tells that in 1940s Liverpool, he slept five to a bed on a mattress 'full of vermin'. Then we see clips from *Housing Problems*, a film sponsored by the Gas Board, made by Edgar Anstey in 1935, on poverty in London. The Gas Board were at that point making minor investments into social housing, such as the Kensal House set of functionalist flats in West London, which would appear on one 'Your Britain – Fight for It Now' poster in 1943. Other footage – a tracking shot across an industrial town – comes from Paul Rotha's 1948 film *Land of Promise*, a thumpingly assertive propaganda tract in support of the welfare state.

The selection and the edit of the excerpts are strange. They are sourced from different places and different times, united only by the political fervour of the director. For example, we cut to footage of Labour's leader in the 1930s, George Lansbury, giving a speech. He's denouncing bankers, with biblical fervour and a strong London accent. 'You don't make *wealth* by passing around pieces of paper!' He then announces that we are 'marching to the conquest of the future! Marching to build Jerusalem in this green and pleasant land!' Followed by another observation from Sam Watts: 'We had the greatest empire in the world, and we had the worst slums in Europe.' Tony Benn's instantly recognisable voice then recalls that workers of his acquaintance during the war wanted to know why, since we can produce machinery to kill Germans, why not to build homes and hospitals? On screen appear extracts from the Labour Party Manifesto of 1945, telling us that 'The Labour Party is a socialist party and proud of it. Its ultimate goal is the establishment of the socialist commonwealth of Great Britain.' And over it all, a brass band plays 'Jerusalem'.

There is a moving depiction of the setting-up of the National Health Service, replacing a system in which, one of the many doctors interviewed in the film tells us, 'the doctor would double up as a debt collector.' The minister of health, Aneurin Bevan, ensured that 'everything which looked like a hospital was nationalised', and services were free at the point of use.

The railways are taken over too, and all public transport is nationalised – haulage, roads, ports, canals, the lot. A more critical note is introduced in the section on these nationalised industries. At first, miners are described as being in tears as the pits are taken into public ownership: 'We've got control of our own lives', something they had been demanding for decades, including in the long, bitter industrial actions of 1926 that triggered a brief General Strike. Herbert Morrison, the minister who created those industries, is seen speaking of this 'great experiment', this 'great adventure' in socialism. But the miners interviewed recall their horror that pre-war coal barons were appointed at the head of the new Coal Board. Dockers, to give another example, now had a legal minimum of daily work, but were still essentially casual labourers. The film then splices in optimistic footage of new estates, New Towns, and the 1951

Festival of Britain. Then, suddenly, like a shift into nightmare: Thatcher!

One could pick holes in *The Spirit of '45* – everything that happened between 1951 and 1979 is largely ignored, as of course is the Empire. This does all miss the point a little, which is that Loach is determined to make an argument, and everything is subordinated to it. Basically, in 1945, a welfare state – flawed, to be sure – was set up to ensure that the poverty and inequality of pre-war Britain never returned; and from 1979 onwards, those institutions were dismantled one by one, leaving just the carcass of the National Health Service. Nothing is superfluous to this single, relentless point. It makes an appeal: *You, or your grandparents, built something hugely important. Don't let them destroy it.*

One of the younger interviewees, the socialist economist James Meadway, notes that Churchill's counter-attack against the rising tide of social democracy was to distribute copies of Friedrich Hayek's tract *The Road to Serfdom*, and to argue that the promised new institutions would have to be administered by a Gestapo. He was ridiculed. In 1979, Thatcher would fling copies of Hayek's books at cabinet ministers and intone 'This is what we believe.'

The last few minutes of the film condense Thatcher's assault on the welfare state – the sell-off of utilities, the recasualisation of the docks, the sell-off of the railways; clips of miners being pummelled by police. Everything stays in monochrome, but the footage is, by now, from the last few years, as we're told that the NHS is the last survival, crippled by part-privatisation and new bureaucracies. We see 'Save the NHS' placards, then we see images from recent

Occupy protests, and UK Uncut. That brass rendition of 'Jerusalem' plays over the footage of their camps. Then, suddenly, we see that same frolicking celebration at VE day on Trafalgar Square in colour. The trick is clear. Look at these joyous young people, how happy and confident they are. They achieved something incredible. So could we.

The populism of *The Spirit of '45*, when combined with the fierceness of its political argument and the wit and venom of the elderly interviewees, is not at all a bad thing. It is moving, sentimental, and that's as it should be; it's a film about hugely emotional events.

The problem lies elsewhere, in what Walter Benjamin in the 1920s called 'left-wing melancholy'. When watching all this footage, seeing these people doing these things, hearing this insurgent language and knowing about the real improvement in real lives that ensued, you're also enjoying the beauty of the chimney-striped skylines, the shabby elegance of an un-cleaned Trafalgar Square, the sense of someone else's possibility. Accompanied by the relentless call of brass bands, the effect is as prone to make you sigh with wistfulness as it is to make you want to hang Eric Pickles from the nearest lamp-post.

And here is where the whiteness of the film, its sidestepping of that 'greatest Empire in the world', matters.[3] If this is an attempt to convince people here and now to defend what's left of the welfare state, it seems odd to use an iconography so firmly rooted in a past that so much of the contemporary working class had nothing to do with. Brass bands and union banners are so alien to most of those who *right now* have the power in their hands to change things, it could as well be a depiction of the English Revolution of the seventeenth century. The decision to bleach out the colour of the contemporary footage makes even today's arguments look melancholic and wistful. The attempt to set up a link between, say, Clement Attlee and UK Uncut is defeated by assimilating the aesthetics of the latter to the former.

That's even more true with the next example of leftist austerity nostalgia.

To Benn or Not to Benn

The poster for Skip Kite's 2014 documentary *Will and Testament* is a take-off of the 'Keep Calm and Carry On' poster – same font, same red. But below the title, the avuncular figure of pipe-smoker, tea-drinker, reluctant aristocrat, Christian Socialist and the most important and influential serious left-wing politician in Britain since 1960, the late Anthony Wedgwood Benn.

Those of us who marched, or rather shuffled, against the Iraq war through freezing London streets in February 2003 on the way to hear Benn speak in Hyde Park will remember a placard which emerged from seemingly nowhere, with the slogan 'MAKE TEA, NOT WAR', featuring Tony Blair holding a machine gun with an upturned teacup on his head. It really was genuinely funny the first time. It displayed a breezy, self-deprecating, 'typically English wit' similar to the Keep Calm poster. Benn's liking for strong tea – he was once informed that he drank enough to kill a horse – makes the juxtaposition rather apt, but highlights the problem at the heart of the film.

That is, the failure to wrest the man's political radicalism from his aesthetic cosiness. In the first scenes of the film, an actor playing Benn sits in a room surrounded by press headlines, mostly vitriolic – 'The Most Dangerous Man in Britain', 'Benn the Dictator' – and then a voice describes him as 'admired by all shades of opinion'. A little while later, Benn, interviewed in 2013, recalls his relief at receiving a death threat for the first time in years – a sign that for some, at least, he wasn't a National Treasure. 'I was so chuffed!'

Will and Testament has a similar format to *The Spirit of '45*, and in many cases reprises the exact same documentary clips from the 1930s and 40s. Moving in chronological order, it avoids the overarching, propagandistic voiceovers of its source material. Instead, it proceeds via extracts from in-depth interviews with Benn interspersed with clips from the era and occasional splices from a feature film (such as the notorious exposition of the neoliberal creed in Paddy Chayefsky's media satire *Network*). There are odd little filmed clips of a small boy running through a Blitzed London, and a stand-in Benn who watches old Super-8 home movies, which probably the actual Benn, a widower from his wife, the American educationalist and historian Caroline Benn, might have found a little too much. To accuse a film about a very old man, missing his wife, defeated in his politics, of being too melancholic is obviously unfair – how could it be anything else?

The film does attempt to explain what Benn's politics were, how they were shaped, and how they were defeated. Formative lessons are learnt from his Christian Socialist mother: 'she taught me that the real questions were moral questions', while the Bible was conveyed to to him as the battle of 'Prophets versus Kings'. The Blitz comes next, 'a sense that the whole world was coming to an end'; 'I had my real education during the war', he tells us, not so much because it shifted him to the left (his father was a Labour MP) as through meeting non-aristocratic people for the first time.

And here, unlike in *Spirit of '45*, we're made aware of colonialism, as Benn the airman recalls how he learned to fly in 'what was then South Rhodesia', and saw that 'none of what we'd call human rights' were enjoyed by the masses. 'Colonial liberation was only one stage of the process' to get freedom here. He recalls his early membership of CND. Through all of this the director or Benn or both are making him sound a lot more radical than he actually was, a centrist Labour MP elected in 1950 to a seat in Bristol as the 'baby of the house'.

The imagery often wins out over the narrative, another ragbag of nostalgic bites. Benn giving a barnstorming speech made to empty green benches. Benn listening to an old radio – the sort likely to sell for a good sum at an austerity-nostalgia market – on which Sir Laurence Olivier is reading out the founding charter of the United Nations. Hugh Dalton plummily expounding on the need to tax the rich, and using the war as superb moral blackmail. Brass bands and nationalised industries in black and white. Prefabs being put together, just as warships and planes had been. An election float: 'Smash the slums with LABOUR'. All these juxtapositions begin to seem outright slapdash, a disorganised procession of signifiers: 'Our Democracy', 'Our Great Past', 'The Good Old Days When Politics Really Mattered'.

This is a shame, as the Benn story – particularly from the early 1970s to the early 80s, when he shifted sharply to the left and became the unofficial leader of the Labour Opposition – is a fascinating and important one. Here, it is fudged in favour of a gauzy wash of Durham Miners' Gala melancholia.

Benn's started out as a technocrat, presiding over the White Heat of Technology as postmaster general and creator of 'Mintech'. He speaks of the beauty of the glass skyscraper of Millbank Tower (which would be menaced by student protesters in 2010), of how technology will help us 'do more with less'. The nostalgia is now of a futurist sort – automation, computers, Concorde. Recalling this time, he is contrite about nuclear power (a believer in 'atoms for peace', he was shocked when he realised that Sellafield and the rest were basically 'bomb factories for the Pentagon'), and dismisses Concorde as a pointless project, when in aviation 'the future was mass transport' rather than record-breaking. There's only a sliver on the discovery of North Sea Oil, when Benn pushed – and failed to convince the cabinet – for the establishment of a Norwegian-style nationalised fund from the profits, something which helped that country become the richest in the world. Thatcher used the revenue 'to pay for the dole and tax cuts', not for the industrial investment and restructuring Benn wanted. In response to all this he becomes the Benn we know, speaking at the Upper Clyde Shipbuilders work-in to demand workers' control, and developing the – here unexplored – Alternative Economic Strategy against the austerity regime imposed on the Callaghan government by the IMF.

This brief engagement with real points of possibility, none of them familiar, dissipates into a montage of Thatcher, Toxteth and Tebbit, to the sound of The Beat's 'Stand Down Margaret'. The Labour civil war that Benn fought valiantly and lost utterly is totally ignored, and the Miners' Strike – save for a striking clip of Benn denouncing media manipulation live on ITN – is merely a cue for more brass bands and mournful marches.

In 1983 Benn lost his southern seat, and subsequently took one in a mining town in Derbyshire. The rest follows a powerless politician who's doing his level best, promising a better future to a mostly grey-haired audience, reading W. H. Auden's 'Funeral Blues', and telling us that 'austerity means the poor paying for the banks gambling with their money'. It also means these images bolstering up our defeated and demoralised side with stuff that makes us feel warm inside, adding up to a fond evocation of simpler days *when it all meant something*.

At the end, he gazes out over the channel, with pipe and cardie, musing on how 'the alternative is socialism or barbarism'. He's right, and sure, he's heroic, but the upshot is a feeling that 'we shall never see his like again'. This is not a call to arms but a disarming eulogy before the politician takes his place in the pantheon of Great Britishers, defused and defanged.

Against the Condescension of Posterity

In *Our Hidden Lives*, an anthology of Mass Observation diaries of the late 1940s, George Taylor, an enthusiastic member of the local Workers Educational Association, describes an unusual new programme. At the Association's monthly executive committee meeting, he notes that 'as an experiment, next year, we are having a class on Appreciation of the Films, and a most attractive syllabus has been drawn up. The committee members are a little afraid, however, that the class may be used for entertainment purposes only, and they have fixed a class fee of 10/- to emphasise that serious study is intended.'[4] People might not be paying full attention – they might turn up just to be titillated and excited, rather than edified. There's little risk of this in Scottish artist Luke Fowler's film on the WEA, *The Poor Stockinger, the Luddite Cropper and the Deluded Followers of Joanna Southcott*.

The Poor Stockinger is, however, unusual in the company of *Will and Testament* or *The Spirit of '45*. Not only because it's not a populist documentary but a consciously avant-garde work, distributed to art galleries rather than for sale for a fiver in Fopp or on Netflix. It's also unusual because the majority of its footage is of the British landscape today, rather than archival clips. Its subject is the work of E. P. Thompson, whose focus on the deep roots of English radical movements and the importance for the left of the enduring notion of the 'free-born Englishman' has been influential on the likes of Billy Bragg and 'Blue Labour'. Thompson thus belongs with Attlee, Orwell and co in the pantheon of the consciously English, patriotic left –

though clearly his own politics were far more stringent. Specifically, Fowler's film focuses on Thompson's activity with the Workers' Educational Association (WEA, an adult education body founded in 1903) in the 1950s, when the situation as described is a great deal bleaker than one would expect. This exploration of socialist ideas in everyday life in the post-war era is far removed from the usual nostalgic narrative.

Fowler's film is simple enough in its approach. The artist Cerith Wyn Evans reads Thompson's notes on teaching at branches of the WEA across the West Riding of Yorkshire; meanwhile the screen shows archival footage and present-day static-camera images of the same area. Wyn Evans's halting, if full-voiced readings, and the often melancholy colour of the images – it's hard *not* to look West Yorkshire in the face without a certain lachrymosity creeping in – make it seem at first like an elegiac film, a film about something which no longer exists. However, traces of hope do emerge from within it.

The title derives from Thompson's trenchant introduction to *The Making of the English Working Class, 1780–1832*, where he explains a methodological break with how Marxist history had hitherto been practised. Rather than charting the origins of working-class political movements which bore obvious fruit in the present, instead he would take seriously the hopes, lives, dreams, statements and quirks of those who actually did exist. Thus rioters and looters, Luddites, religious sectarians, putsch-initiating ultra-left Jacobins, all were to be rescued from the 'enormous condescension of posterity' and discovered in their totality as thinking, acting people and collectives, that made their own history as much as they were made by the forces ranged against them.

It's impossible for anyone to watch the film without thinking of Thompson's most famous book. It appears at a double, or triple, remove: the early proletariat that Thompson is teaching lessons about; the mill-workers, miners, retirees and clerks that he's teaching to; and the flashes of a present-day proletariat we see loitering outside the disused or dilapidated shells of old schools, colleges and factories. Do the people Thompson listed as patronised by the 'condescension of posterity' – the 'poor stockinger, the Luddite cropper, the "obsolete" hand-weaver, the "utopian" artisan, and even the deluded followers of Joanna Southcott' – have their later correspondents in any of these? In the call-centre worker, the single mother, the ex-miner on the sick, the Nestlé factory operative, the occupier of the Westfield hole in Bradford, the Huddersfield SolFed anarchist, the Leeds Islamist?

This raises the question – without mawkish nostalgia – of what the working class today actually consists of.

Thompson's great insight as a historian was always to write about the working class as it was, rather than as he would have wished it to be, the ideal proletariat with 'imputed class consciousness', in György Lukács's phrase. Yet many of his contemporaries in English Marxism contended that he wasn't able to do this in the present. Instead, they argued, he overstated the influence of radical socialism and communism in the British Isles, and erected a consolatory image of World War II as a missed prelude to revolution. In his book, set between the 1780s and the 1830s, Thompson tells the story of how the the politically active working class shifted from the 'God and King Mob' – the proudly patriotic and reactionary force that broke up radical meetings and marches, loudly asserting its solidarity with its oppressors – into the active, conscious, autonomous, self-educating force of Luddism and the Swing Riots, utopian 'Owenism' and then Chartism.

For Blue Labour and the like, the working class remains the God and King Mob, whose prejudices must be appealed to – a fiction, concocted out of a half-truth called 'the white working class'. This narrative proposes that the working class are simple folk, disinclined to do too much in the way of thinking, who might trot out to wave a flag for the Jubilee, but otherwise care little for the world outside of their 'communities'. Hence they resent people from an 'alien culture' moving over here and taking their jobs and their council houses. The argument continues, therefore, that because they are, alas, the majority of the population, politicians have no choice but to listen to their grievances.

An early essay in this line is Michael Collins's *The Likes of Us: A Biography of the White Working Class*, which was essentially a biography of the God and King Mob in a small corner of South-East London. For Collins, the 'white working class' is a 'forgotten tribe', an ethnicity, best defined by its 'culture' – accent, manners, clothes, tastes and traditions, all regularly scoffed at by a coalition of liberals, lefties and ethnics.

A working-class upbringing is an alibi for life, so that no matter how much wealth and property the ex-prole might accumulate, no matter how smartly he or she has kicked the ladder from below them, they will still doggedly describe themselves as 'working-class'. This is the inverse of Thompson's approach. He defines 'working-class' in the preface to *The Making* less as a fixed sociological category or immovable structure than as 'something that happens to people', a constantly shifting, warping condition that works as a process, with advances and defeats.

The problem with this, at least for Thompson's critics, is that when writing about the post-war era, he took for granted an imputed class consciousness in ways that were increasingly absurd; that he failed to follow his own precepts in treating class as mutable. In 'The Myths of Edward Thompson', part of a heated argument about England's 'incomplete bourgeois revolution', Perry Anderson poured scorn on Thompson's reckless overstatements of the scope and influence of English Marxism, which led him to the bathetic claim that communism was, in a fittingly West Yorks metaphor, some sort of Heathcliff in the Labour movement's *Wuthering Heights*. Anderson claimed that when looking at the working class of the present, Thompson could only see that of the past: 'the divorce between his intimacy and concord with the late 18th and early 19th centuries, and his distance and lack of touch with the second half of the 20th century, is baffling. It is a divorce that is evidently rooted deep in the sensibility'. The composition of the working class – who they are, what they do for a living, where the political fault lines might lie – is increasingly ignored, in favour of a vague, windy, imprecise notion of 'The People' – and 'who the "common people" are is never said:

they exist only as figments in this moralistic rhetoric. The fact that the majority of the population in England in this period voted consistently for Conservative governments is brushed aside.'[5]

The reasons for this are less opaque in the reports read out in *The Poor Stockinger*, as the connection between past movements and present, largely working-class, students is extraordinarily close. Past experience lurks constantly in the background, a memory of suffering and struggle that the older students are constantly able to draw upon. This might have something to do with the intensely local focus of Thompson's activities, and of the film itself. Fowler documents some of the places where the Independent Labour Party was born – precisely those areas most overlooked by historians, those most subject to the condescension of posterity, as much as they are subject to condescension in the present. 'The ILP grew from the bottom up', writes Thompson in his 'Homage to Tom Maguire',

> its birthplaces were in those shadowy parts known as 'the provinces'. It was created by the fusing of local elements into one national whole. From the circumference its members came to establish the centre. Its first council seat was won in the Colne Valley: its first authentic parliamentary challenges came in Bradford and Halifax: its first conference showed an overwhelming preponderance of strength in the North of England: its early directories show this strength consolidated. When the two-party political structure began to crack, and a third party with a distinctively socialist character emerged, this occurred [not] in Westminster but amongst the mills, brickyards and gasworks of the West Riding.[6]

Fowler's film is a meditation about this place a century later, as well as a film about the relationship between education and class. It begins with footage of E. P. Thompson on a television discussion programme, talking about William Blake's poem 'London'. Much hinges on a change in the poem, from the early drafts where London's streets were 'dirty', to the final version, where the poet 'wanders through each chartered street' – one of the first analyses, in its brief, elliptical, allusive way, of a new urban capitalism. What we see isn't London, though. The 'chartered streets' are car parks, empty hotel rooms. A building appears on screen – the Bradford and Bingley headquarters in Bingley, a brutalist ziggurat designed for the Mutual in the early 1970s by John Brunton and Partners.

The allusive structure of the film hinges on these kinds of moments, where you have to pick up quickly the implications of seemingly innocent shots. The Bingley building represents the civic modernism of the period that the film partly deals with, albeit a bureaucratic modernism that Thompson would hardly have been in sympathy with. You see its confidence, scale and topographical drama – and you're reminded of the current crisis, where Bradford and Bingley were one of the first financial institutions to have been nationalised by Gordon Brown's government.[7] Their total embrace of the new, electronic, immaterial high finance nearly destroyed them. This North is no longer a landscape of production, but one of speculation.

What has this to do with Thompson's text, 'Against University Standards', now being read out by Cerith Wyn Evans with alternate precision and start-stop faltering?

The text proposes a militant form of education. Could that help us to interpret this landscape politically?

From here on in, the film centres on Thompson's WEA reports, beginning with Cleckheaton in 1951, where the 'paucity of the book box' means that it's difficult to have students even read the designated texts. What we see are the flickering lights of the hilly mill town, and what we hear is Thompson noting that the class was roused to its most heated discussion when debating the degeneration of pattern design, after the change from hand-weaving to machine-weaving. A political question merges with an aesthetic question, as the machine-weavers themselves ponder the machine's inability to reproduce the care of hand-design.

The scene moves to Batley, where we see a neo-gothic school, a dilapidated Fox's Biscuits factory, an empty classroom and an advertisement asking if you have been 'mis-sold PPI'. This is juxtaposed with Thompson admitting defeat after one of his students starts 'thumping the table in defence of Gladstone's integrity', and the others go on to share irrelevant local memories, and the teacher/agitator loses control. Thompson ruefully notes that there's no point in fulminating against the students for not being what they never claimed to be.

This sense of melancholia and failure lifts a little when the scene moves to Halifax, where Thompson is giving his 1954–55 report on the Social History class. Thompson talks of trying to cajole his students out of seeing 'social history as a long-winded preface to the welfare state'.

In Bradford, the number of different voices suddenly increases – rather than just hearing Thompson's reports, we hear some of those who were WEA students, talking about how he was equally as interested in bird-watching as in Marx's political economy. Another recalls a class on strikes in Leeds. Another that 'we saw it as part of the battle between left and right in the Labour movement'. A counter-voice says, 'I think it's a dead end, having classes open to everybody and expecting it to be university standard', and another unnamed voice notes the suspicion the WEA was held in among the 'official' universities. The very nature of the working class was changing, comments someone. Were these classes part of a dying culture?

Few clues are offered at the film's end in Leeds, among its green-domed new mosques, its wasted industrial estates and pristine Portland stone university buildings. In an elliptical, disjointed way, it feels as if the film has done something to re-establish those 'lines of communication' that are otherwise lost. It finds recessed in a dismal present a tradition that is not – quite – dead. But as the shots of Leeds's busy, ill-thought-out landscape fade into each other, the question will have to be answered elsewhere – what would a radical education for *this* place be like? Even a work as intelligent and conscientious as this, as determined to avoid the easy tropes of left-wing melancholy, ends up creating a picture of the present as a landscape of desolation.

In the face of the somewhat false, retrospective optimism of *The Spirit of '45* or *Will and Testament*, the astringent, rigorous refusal to come to easy conclusions or make facile links between our problems and those of the past in *The Poor Stockinger* seems particularly admirable. Here, the post-war decades are not something we leap over to get from the joyous liberation of 1945 to the malevolent counter-revolution of 1979, but a complex, difficult, dialectical moment, when the industrial working-class culture to which Benn devoted the last years of his life was already passing away, even before its violent murder in 1984. There is absolutely nothing in *The Poor Stockinger* that Blue Labour could find useful, and its approach to the familiar subject matter of austerity nostalgia is totally devoid of the usual formal tropes – no Gill Sans, no Radiophonic Workshop, no We Love Our NHS. However, it's telling that this more subtle approach to the subject is confined to the art circuit. Fowler has the luxury here of not being expected to make an argumentative point, to convince you that things were better before, that something was lost, that here's what we do next. Nothing is reconciled in this film. Because *reconciliation* is what this is all really about. All this discussion of a nostalgia for the way that, back in the 1940s, it seemed possible to reconcile patriotism and socialism, misses one rather odd fact: this was, even then, a conscious construction, one which faced a fair degree of opposition. The austerity that we are nostalgic about was *already* nostalgic, and its modernity was an attempt to reconcile apparently incompatible things – modernity and tradition, the urban and the rural, avant-garde design and the arts and crafts. It is to that original invention of the austerity aesthetic tradition that we must now turn.

3

The Aesthetic Empire of Ingsoc

In the eighteenth century a high standard of design was set by the cul-
tivated taste of an aristocracy. Though our modern bureaucracy, which
acts in the same capacity, has not yet succeeded in acquiring definite
enough standards of its own to exert a similar influence, we have had
the benefit of some equivalent; namely that of certain big public and
industrial corporations, notably the London Transport Board, whose
influence on design in the inter-war years was incalculable.

J. M. Richards, *Modern Architecture* (1940)[1]

With the wave of austerity nostalgia there naturally comes
a history to match. The best-selling revision of design
history fit for stocking in the local branch of Cath Kidston
is Alexandra Harris's *Romantic Moderns*. If Ghost Box and
their ilk make up their retrospective construction through
Stonehenge, comprehensive schools, Penguin design,
the BBC Radiophonic Workshop, the Central Office of
Information, Arthur Machen and BBC Ghost Stories,

then Harris's beautifully produced, original and very successful book throws together Stonehenge, stately homes,
Cornish villages, John Piper, Paul Nash, Edward Bawden
and Eric Ravilious, László Moholy-Nagy, Cecil Beaton,
Bill Brandt and Virginia Woolf. It is a scholarly text rather
than a pop-culture assemblage, but similarly is about historical revisionist wish-fulfilment. What, ask Ghost Box,
if the real pop-culture crazes of the 1960s and 70s weren't
rock and its permutations but the public modernism of state
and para-state institutions? What, Alexandra Harris asks,
if modernism wasn't really about the transformation of
space, the destruction of slums and their replacement with
something better for the working class, the overcoming of
the nineteenth century and its physical legacy – but instead
an upper-class movement about the rediscovery of roots?
This thesis has just enough truth to be convincing, and
to make it a sort of art-historical adjunct to the Ravilious
print, the Mumford & Sons record and the Keep Calm and
Carry On tea towel.

Harris's book is best summarised by the review in *The
Chap*, a bi-monthly journal whose blend of knowingly
absurd mock-aristocratic posing, knowingly unrecon-
structed chauvinism (that flesh you're gazing at is ironic
burlesque, not *Nuts* magazine) and knowingly stupid upper-
class mannerisms has been surprisingly popular, launching
a thousand East London moustaches. Sharing a page with
Kiss Me, Chudleigh! The World According to Auberon Waugh
and *Empire of the Clouds – When Britain's Aircraft Ruled the
World*, our reviewer tells us that 'while hardcore modernism was about stark architecture and minimal abstraction,

the romantic modernists lauded the delights of country churches, gypsy-caravans and hedgerows. Ms Harris rescues them from their pigeonhole as quaint and fusty eccentrics ... [and] makes one think again about what it is to be British.'[2] Having a good think about what it is to be British is a constant in all this stuff. However, what Harris is doing is in many ways more dangerous, given that, unlike Ghost Box's fantasy history, it does bear some relation to historical reality.

She begins by tracing the way painters like John Piper, Graham Sutherland and Paul Nash moved, within a few years in the 1930s, from constructivist-influenced abstraction to a fascination with the English (almost always English) landscape: spaces that can be natural, agricultural, Neolithic or semi-urban, like country towns. 'By the late 1930s', she writes, 'it looked to observers as if a whole concerted project of national self-discovery was underway.'[3] What did this project consist of?

One of her prime examples is the British Pavilion at the 1937 Paris World Expo. This event is best known for three pavilions that spoke eloquently and terrifyingly of the disaster Europe was careering into – the pavilions of the Third Reich and the Soviet Union, flanking the Eiffel Tower, two stone monoliths topped by sculptures, where the heroic workers and peasants of the latter seem to rush into the eagle of the former; and the restrained, modernist Spanish Republic Pavilion, that showcased Picasso's *Guernica* to the public for the first time. The British Pavilion, in that alarming context, stood as an oasis of calm. The architect, Oliver Hill, used laconic forms indebted to Le Corbusier for the

facade, but the exhibits, curated by London Transport director Frank Pick, were full of a warm, reassuring whimsy.
'Packing-case placelessness became home to soil types and
fishing boots and Ravilious's mural of a lawn tennis court',
along with a life-size cut-out of Neville Chamberlain with
a fishing rod.[4]

After a couple of years, despite Chamberlain's valiant
(albeit unmentioned) attempts to divert the two totalitarian
states to fight each other and leave Blighty in peace to play
tennis and go fishing, Britain was roped into the European
war. The Romantic Moderns' response was best encapsulated in the 'Recording Britain' project, curated by Sir
Kenneth Clark, then of the National Gallery. This under-
taking was at the heart of a recent exhibition at Tate Britain,
where striking watercolours of hills, streets, churches and
ruins with all the richly dour, wet, green-brown-purple
of the English landscape were displayed on the walls, to a
recording of the British Jewish pianist Myra Hess playing
Beethoven at the National Gallery during the Blitz. It was
undeniably stirring. Clark commissioned 'one thousand
five hundred topographical watercolours', largely concentrated on the landscapes of the south of England because
'the bombs looked set to obliterate them first'. This was
perhaps spurious, since apart from the Baedeker raids on
cathedral towns, the main targets for the bombs were industrial, working-class areas in London's East End, Liverpool,
Manchester, Coventry, Southampton, Plymouth, Bristol,
Clydeside and Hull. These, the East End aside, appeared to
be missing, but then the project was meant to be 'small in
scale, depicting small-scale things'.[5]

Britain was a safe haven for exiles from the terrible continent, and it changed them at least as much as they changed it. Serge Chermayeff designed himself a contextual country house, Walter Gropius made a village school in Cambridgeshire, Moholy-Nagy photographed Oxford and Petticoat Lane. Even those works which might appear to be indictments of Britain's inequality, hypocrisy and petty cruelties were in fact, for Harris, just a curious continental's eye view. Photographer and Austrian exile Bill Brandt's book, *The English at Home*, where grinding, bug-ridden poverty is juxtaposed with bourgeois and aristocratic comfort in surreal, high-contrast, estranging images, may have been 'a pictorial essay on the gap between rich and poor, but it was also a fond study of the ways people take possession of their environments'.[6]

This bias comes through especially strongly when Harris arrives at the war and its immediate aftermath. Many of her protagonists were working on the projects of the welfare state, some of them extensively; and yet something like Coventry Cathedral, a modernist-gothic collaboration between the camp, decorative Scottish modernist Sir Basil Spence and Romantic Modernists like John Piper and Graham Sutherland, which even incorporates a ruin, is obviously a bit too grey and socialist and municipal for Harris. Clark's wartime watercolours aside, the 1940s appear in *Romantic Moderns* only in relation to the decline of the country house. The laments, with varying degrees of self-awareness, of Edith Sitwell, Evelyn Waugh and Elizabeth Bowen over the fate of the stately home are bafflingly dominant. Waugh and Bowen in particular are

incensed at the dereliction of their birthright by the socialist government, irrespective (or because) of the fact that it
was trying, via the National Trust, to make many stately
homes accessible to the public. Waugh's fulminations are
well known, as is his defence of the institution in *Brideshead
Revisited* – it is only the claim that he was some sort of
modernist that is surprising. The books by this trio on the
fate of the country house were 'campaigns waged against
utility',[7] a target which may have seemed a little bizarre or
even offensive to the hundreds of thousands of people the
new welfare state was enabling to experience utility for the
first time (their first medical treatment, their first homes
with central heating and bathrooms and without vermin
and rot, that sort of thing). However, this project was
evidently unromantic.

The angriest of them all appears to have been the Anglo-
Irish novelist Elizabeth Bowen, whose profile of her family
home in County Cork, *Bowen's Court*, provides the culmination of *Romantic Moderns*. Bowen, via Harris, claims that

> power without an object is uncontainable, which is why, she thinks,
> 'we have everything to dread from the dispossessed'. This is the
> political justification of that deep feeling for ownership and for con-
> tinuity which runs through *Bowen's Court*, a book which starts with
> a map, a long topographical prelude which lays claim to a whole
> stretch of north Cork landscape, and a lover's description of a
> house which has moods and experiences.[8]

At this point, the very large thing not being talked about is
no longer the working class, but the Empire. Quite other

people – animate, thinking people, with their own moods and experiences – might have laid claim to the north Cork landscape. They might have found the assertion that power as exercised by the Anglo-Irish aristocracy was limited, careful and contained to be a dubious one, at best. These people are acknowledged only through the dread they inspired in Bowen after an IRA group occupied Bowen's Court, pondering, and then deciding not to, burn it down like they had so many other 'ascendancy houses' whose blackened remains 'pitted' the Irish landscape after the Irish Civil War. Moving in one sentence from the destructive work of the IRA to the effects of the welfare state, Harris tells us that 'in England, inheritors faced ruinous taxation'.[9] The end of the Empire and the aristocracy are a matter for lament – if only modernism could have formed an alliance with them! The Romantic Moderns who maintained their romanticism are those who, like John Betjeman, devoted the post-war era largely to denouncing the aesthetic effects of the welfare state's building programmes.

By this point, although we're still in the territory of austerity nostalgia, we might seem to be a long way away from the welfare state, which now appears as the adversary of this nostalgia, and no longer its fulfilment. What is most interesting is that public institutions of any sort are invisible in *Romantic Moderns*. Institutions that sponsored modern design, art or architecture like London Transport, the London County Council, the General Post Office, the Ministry of Information and the Empire Marketing Board are all conspicuous by their absence – the only equivalent is the publicity programme of the oil company Shell, which sponsored Guides edited by Betjeman, Nash, Piper and others, and produced gently surreal advertisements from the likes of Nash, Sutherland and Vanessa Bell. The 'public' too are absent, and there is barely a sign of the Great Depression and urban England in general.

However, the erasure of even the mildest social democracy from the record of English modernism is a very contemporary thing to do. Harris created the perfect art history for a country where constant appeals to Keep Calm and Carry On, to the Blitz, the bulldog spirit and what have you, along with the conservation of select pieces of pre- and post-war modernist architecture, coincide with the destruction of the welfare state's last remnants. Compared to that, the close alliance of modernists – even ones that liked country churches and stone circles – with social democracy and socialism can be written out of history without it mattering all that much.

In this, Harris parts company a little with her austerity-nostalgic contemporaries. Most of the fetish objects of austerity nostalgia were either produced by, or are imitations of, the products of certain institutions, companies and nationalised corporations that existed in Britain roughly between 1930 and 1970. The London County Council (LCC), for example, created out of the inner London boroughs in the 1890s and wound up into the less powerful, larger Greater London Council (GLC) in the 1960s, before that in turn was abolished in the 1980s. The London Passenger Transport Board (LPTB, or 'London Transport'), created out of the 1933 nationalisation of the privately owned Underground Group. The Ministry of Information, later spawning the

Central Office of Information, a governmental propaganda body especially active during the war. The GPO (General Post Office, i.e. Royal Mail), whose Film Unit produced a remarkable body of work in the 1930s before being transformed during the war into the Crown Film Unit, under the command of the Ministry of Information. And finally there's the Festival of Britain, the celebratory event where all these came together in 1951 as a 'tonic for the nation' on a Thames-side site, most of its structures later demolished by the newly elected Conservative government as 'three-dimensional socialist propaganda'.

The Tube posters that we find today, with their slightly sinister authoritarian modernism, are ironic borrowings from the real posters produced by the LPTB. The films of Ken Loach and Skip Kite evoke GPO/Crown films like *Night Mail* and *Listen to Britain*. The brick architecture of contemporary London evokes the tenements produced en masse by the LCC in the interwar years. The Festival has been a sourcebook for dozens of gee-gaws, gadgets, posters, notebooks, tea towels, models and suchlike. And, as we have seen, the 'Keep Calm and Carry On' poster was an unreleased product of the Ministry of Information.

Unlike that poster, however, most of these institutions were very real and left a permanent mark on Britain, especially upon London and its encircling commuter belt. But delve a little into the architectural, design and film work of these bodies and you find that they, too, were driven by an exceptionally powerful nostalgia. All of them were working against the dread of an incipient Americanised consumer society, the 'by-pass England' that J. B. Priestley found on his 1934 *English Journey*. This was a new nation marked by 'glass and concrete and chromium plate', its art deco factories turning out 'potato crisps, scents, tooth pastes, bathing costumes, fire extinguishers',[10] made up of 'arterial and by-pass roads, of filling stations and factories that look like exhibition buildings, of giant cinemas and dance-halls and cafes, cocktail bars, Woolworths, factory girls looking like actresses'.[11]

As an alternative to such a consumer society, these democratic yet deeply mandarin bodies harked back to the mirage of a democratic yet deferent and decorous England (seldom Scotland or Wales) that they imagined had once existed. They found this fancied England largely among the working class that was then flocking to the Odeons and the by-pass retail centres.

Although seldom treated historically as one bloc – except of course in the ironic-authoritarian-consumerist dreamworld of austerity nostalgia – this peculiar form of

The architecture of interwar consumerism: Hoover Factory, Perivale

benevolent, Fabian-nostalgic-democratic-modernism was actually created by a small group of interconnected people, based in London (though frequently of northern extraction), and male.

The London County Council's head for much of the 1930s, Herbert Morrison, was the main organiser and sponsor of the London Passenger Transport Board, which provided the model for the nationalised industries that he created as home secretary post-1945. The flaws of that model – the need to turn a profit, the lack of workplace democracy – began with the LPTB, as did its virtues of coherence, planning and the creation of visual and social order. Minister Morrison was also the main governmental patron of the Festival of Britain, which he insisted upon against reluctant colleagues.

The LPTB's managing director, the Lincoln-born Frank Pick, shared power in the organisation with the American businessman Lord Ashfield. Pick, however, is better remembered, mainly because of his sponsorship of a massive programme of Tube and bus expansion, whose elegant, bright and apparently 'quintessentially English' stations were designed in an ever more articulate modernist style by Charles Holden, an unorthodox classical architect from Bolton. Pick was also in charge of the poster designs for the enterprise, commissioning work from all the major British and often European artists of the day – a dizzying list including E. McKnight Kauffer, Moholy-Nagy, Man Ray, John Piper, Paul Nash, Graham Sutherland and Abram Games. Pick's career culminated in the late 1930s with the curation of the British Pavilion at the Paris Expo of 1937, followed by an appointment as director general of the wartime Ministry of Information, where he lasted for a mere four months, horrified by the unscrupulous demands of producing wartime propaganda. He died in 1941.

The director general designate of the Ministry of Information, the civil servant Stephen Tallents, was best known for founding the GPO Film Unit in the 1930s, giving great creative freedom to Soviet and German-influenced directors and producers such as John Grierson, Paul Rotha, Basil Wright, Humphrey Jennings, Len Lye and Robert Flaherty. Later Tallents sat on the board of the Festival of Britain, commissioning its logo from Tube poster designer Abram Games.

The Ministry of Information itself was located during the war in Senate House, an icy, stripped-down classical skyscraper designed by Charles Holden, originally for the University of London. This in turn had been commissioned by William Beveridge, the Liberal thinker whose 'Report' in 1943 is the founding document of the post-war welfare state. And nearly all of these thinkers, architects, artists, filmmakers and bureaucrats were involved with a body which is much less often discussed, and whose work has strangely not made it onto iPhone covers and notebooks – the Empire Marketing Board. The EMB had been set up to encourage British consumers to buy products from the distant provinces of an increasingly protectionist (and, with the acquisition of much of the Ottoman Empire in the inter-war years, ever-larger) global Empire.

This list does not exhaust the catalogue of the raw materials of Austerity Nostalgia Mark I. The more aesthetically conservative (in this era at least) BBC is an essential source; at the same time, the entirely private but clearly 'educational' publisher Penguin Books, the autodidact's favourite, sits on its fringes. And not to be forgotten is the era's alternately sympathetic and bitterly ironic chronicler, George Orwell, a marginal figure at the time, but one through whom most of this period is now read.

So what sort of Britain were these people trying to create, and why has it re-emerged so strikingly during twenty-first-century austerity?

The New Jerusalem Underground

In an early essay in the austerity nostalgia genre, the architecture critic Jonathan Glancey held up the LCC, the Festival of Britain and most of all London Transport as worn but still visible beacons of civic purpose within a city crazed by useless 'circuses'. These institutions were in contrast to the Millennium Dome (now the O2), the British Museum Great Court, and the Blairite matrix that would, years later, lead the entire city to be permanently loomed over by a supertall glass Shard, owned by Qatari investors. All this, Glancey told us, would have horrified the people that built interwar (and the first decade or so of post-war) London. These temples of Blairism represented 'the antithesis of the old London County Council's stuffy, patronising, intelligent-design-and-decent-public-services-are-good-for-you approach when London was run by socialists and liberals, and school exercise books were emblazoned with the LCC crest.'[12]

Instead, Glancey asked his reader to remember the legacy of 'the honest and principled man who is one of London's great unsung heroes',[13] Frank Pick: 'Whether you hailed from Stepney or South Kensington, Arnos Grove or Amersham, Pick believed you should be treated equally and well.'[14] It is ironic that this attack on a city treated as a series of trinkets would later become a sourcebook for a new rash of rather more chic and austere-looking trinkets.

The most prominent organisation to be plundered by austerity nostalgia is the London Passenger Transport Board. For historian Michael T. Saler, the Underground was a form of 'medieval modernism', which connected Ruskin to the Bauhaus: 'the culminating project of the arts and crafts movement – a work of public art that united modern painting, sculpture and architecture into a glorious *Gesamtkunstwerk*, a thing of joy to its makers and users'.[15] That's quite a claim; however, no explanation of the strange appeal of austerity nostalgia today can be written without discussing the successes and failures at the time of Pick's remarkable attempt to rationalise London through its underground railway.

London, insisted Frank Pick, has hitherto been an 'accident', and 'no one person has formed it'. But by the 1920s, he proposed, 'it is certain that the future of London cannot be an accident, like in the past ... it must now be planned, designed, and organised.'[16] If it was, it was largely thanks to him. Unlike the many figures dragged out of their post-1960s graves by the austerity-nostalgia industry (formerly forgotten illustrators like Ravilious and Bawden, photographers like Edwin Smith), London Transport's place in design history has long been secure, although the scope of the project is perhaps only now coming home to us, through the sheer proliferation of coffee-table poster books and postcards available via the London Transport Museum shop.

Pick, a scholarship boy educated in York, was initially a publicity man, and rose through the Underground Group – a conglomerate of several private underground lines, built or bought up by the corrupt American 'robber baron' Charles Tyson Yerkes[17] – on the basis of his spectacular success at creating a corporate identity. One of Pick's first acts as managing director of the Underground was to commission the typographer Edward Johnston to create a sans serif typeface, whose unusual combination of legibility, sharpness and friendliness was conspicuous in the disordered streetscape of the Edwardian city.

Even this typeface, with its little diamond dot above the lower-case I, could be – and was – seen to embody a

The signage of London Underground

particular British approach to modernity, a matter of industrial clarity coupled with warmth, even whimsy. The same could be said of the famous 'roundel' logo, where the word 'UNDERGROUND' or just the station name occupied a blue bar across the middle of a red circle, to symbolise the 'Tube' tunnels themselves.

These innovations were followed by a series of poster campaigns, a rationalisation of all stations to limit advertising and clutter, and then several extensions, largely of the Northern, Central and Piccadilly lines of the Underground, with new stations by Charles Holden or his close collaborators. The sum total of this effort, uniting fine art, industrial design, architecture and engineering, leads Michael Saler to call the Underground Group, and from 1933 the LPTB, interwar England's only real avant-garde, a bona fide 'art into life' movement such as the UK didn't otherwise have.

This is not, unlike the construction of *Romantic Moderns*, a matter of anachronistic hindsight; Pick's contemporaries saw it in much the same way. Nikolaus Pevsner praised Pick as a 'Maecenas', and Holden's Tube stations as 'an excellent set of designs, which did so much to establish the modern idiom in Britain. Modest, functional, yet not without elegance', with 'the same elements everywhere slightly modified – the right mixture of standardisation and variation'.[18]

His colleague, *Architectural Review* editor J. M. Richards, noted in 1940 the way in which these stations – which had been 'placed in instructive contrast in the middle of the worst bogus Tudor housing estates' – were 'the most satisfactory series of modern buildings in England', notable for the way that everything, from the bins to the signs to the typography of the timetables was all coordinated as a total design. Its posters, he notes, 'were celebrated all over the world', where 'many of the ideas of modern art – cubism, abstract design, surrealism – are employed on posters and liked by the man in the street'.[19] This all adds up to the remarkable picture of a perfect bureaucracy driving forward a public-spirited corporation.

As managing director of the Underground Group, Pick revolutionised poster design in Britain. When destinations of now notorious suburban tedium – Hatfield, Edgware, Epsom, Ruislip – appeared in posters by E. McKnight Kauffer or Charles Sharland, they were transfigured by wild fauvist colours. They promised the prospective commuter that every day they arrived at the hills on the edge of Pinner, the landscape would glow and pulsate with purples and greens, undulating downs interrupted by little more than a picturesque church spire. The countryside – that the Underground and its stalking gang of speculative house builders would imminently destroy – is always foregrounded as the selling point: a lush, halcyon Rupert Brooke world where time stood still. Here, the poster says, the landscape is as calm, welcoming and undemonstrative as the people. Here there'll *always* be an England.

Placed in the Tube stations of soot-spattered Kennington or Farringdon, these illustrations were a promise that the petit bourgeoisie of London could hardly have been blamed for consuming in droves. The 'modernist' technique – the anti-realistic, sometimes oneiric palette of the painters – was an effective means with which to convey the 'anti-modernist' effect of a timeless rural England just within reach. Less typically, Graham Sutherland's *London Transport Opens a Window on London's Country* looks through a Georgian sash window at a sun-dappled green garden, with a single tree and a hedge beyond. It is unusual not for its modernist/rural style, but for its acknowledgement that the suburban Londoner will be seeing a mere fragment of the countryside beyond his window.

Others were less subtle. Below fauvist or cubist images of rolling fields, tumbledown cottages and medieval churches, appeared slogans like 'Golders Green: A Place of Delightful Prospects'; 'Live in a New Neighbourhood – Dollis Hill'; 'Live in Surrey, Free From Worry'; 'Live in Edgware and LIVE!'[20] It's interesting how little this particular form of imagery features in the austerity-nostalgia world of today, perhaps because these sorts of places, eighty years after they were carpeted with semis, are, with the return of the metropolitan middle classes to the inner city, the very suburbs that graphic designers, restaurateurs and metropolitan movers and shakers actually come from.

Of course, the joys of a new house in Mill Hill or Morden weren't all that the Tube's publicity campaigns relied upon. They also sold the neon lights, theatres, cinemas and department stores of the West End; exhibitions and galleries; the Cup Final at Wembley, the Epsom Derby. Occasionally they just celebrated London in the abstract, especially during and immediately after the war. Accordingly, many Underground Group/London Transport posters are more uncomplicatedly modernist, even surrealist. In one of them, Man Ray twins the Underground roundel and the rings of

Saturn. Interwar work on canvas or using photomontage, by Abram Games, Moholy-Nagy and Hans Schleger, is as bright, dramatic, sharp and metropolitan as anything you could have found at the time in Moscow, Paris or Berlin – as in Moholy-Nagy's remarkable posters proclaiming the joys of escalators and automatic doors and showing you via cutaways how they work. Typical of the contradictions the designers were grappling with is Paul Nash's 'Come Out to Play, Come Out to Live', where he pretends that the suburbs the commuter will return to every evening could be a series of clipped, concrete and glass modernist villas resembling Weimar-era Frankfurt, rather than the mock-Tudor reality.

The Underground buildings, of course, unlike the posters, survive in situ, and can be visited. All stations were subject to a decluttering process insisted upon by Pick from the 1910s onwards. 'Before and After' photographs were a great propaganda tool for the Underground Group/LPTB, showing a mess of ads, tat, trash and poorly coordinated furniture replaced by a smooth, elegant series of wooden kiosks, comfortable, unfussy benches and clear modernist adverts.

Since then much 'recluttering' has occurred, so only a little of this spirit clings on today. Nonetheless, who could fail to become nostalgic upon entering the station at Arnos Grove or Sudbury Town, or Southgate or Cockfosters or Uxbridge or Oakwood? Take the Piccadilly Line northwards, beyond Manor House, and you are in Frank Pick's London, a magical place that doesn't really exist for the denizens of Southwark, Greenwich, Lewisham, Bexley,

Hackney or Newham, who for the most part have to live in Boris Johnson's London.

Despite living in the city for sixteen years, I've lived in 'Frank Pick's London' only when I was house-sitting one Christmas in Hampstead Garden Suburb, the planned utopian community where Pick lived from 1920 until his death in 1941. The area is designed around its square marked only by an 'Institute' (now a girls' school), two churches and a series of Beatrix Potter–style closes and cul-de-sacs, many of them giving way to preserved patches of woodland. Retrogressive, nostalgic, it played at being the country while standing at the heart of what was then the world's largest metropolis. It is still today scrupulously planned and controlled, authoritarian and publess, eccentric and strikingly pretty; it is Pick's ideal city in microcosm, except for the fact its founders made sure it didn't have a Tube. Nonetheless, it is in walking distance from East Finchley station, designed, of course, in the 1930s by Charles Holden.

Sudbury Town, Arnos Grove, Bounds Green and Southgate were the first stations to be opened after the

Frank Pick's London: Hampstead Garden Suburb

Arnos Grove station

early-1930s nationalisation, and hence are unusually well treated, Grade II* listed and officially 'iconic' stations. Step out at Arnos Grove – the best preserved and the least cluttered– and you could be dumbstruck by its austere beauty. The signage on the concrete platforms is the first thing to encounter, in a slightly coarse béton brut, with lots of the signs unchanged since 1933, confident and clear and by now with a patina of heritage chic about them. The ticket hall is truly magnificent – a great concrete drum, held up by a single column, with a futuristic little ticket booth underneath it. Even in rush hour, it gives a remarkable sense of pure space, easy, airy and unpretentious, modern without any shrillness or stridency. Leave the station, and you see behind you a red-brick and concrete building without any classical references that nonetheless feels as serene, ordered, logical and pure as a villa by Inigo Jones.

These Piccadilly Line stations – to the north, they begin at Turnpike Lane, to the west, you start at Boston Manor –

were the culmination of Pick's reform of the London Underground, the Thames-side analogue to heroic infrastructure like the Moscow Metro or the Berlin U-Bahn. The project took over a decade to complete, and it is interesting to track progress from station to station. You find first a gradual hardening of the modernist project, as Pick and Holden come closer to the European modern movement, and then a sudden swing back.

In Europe, from around 1917, various fundamentally similar, if politically and aesthetically diverse movements and bodies – constructivism and suprematism in the USSR, De Stijl and the Amsterdam School in the Netherlands, the Bauhaus in Germany, Le Corbusier and L'Esprit Nouveau in France – all coalesced on a programme of putting elegantly rationalised industrial design, art and architecture at the service of the state. This was grounded in insurrectionary avant-garde movements, in opposition to and scornful of bourgeois values. There was never such a movement in the UK, where the Bloomsbury Group's aesthetic ideas, essentially freezing those of Paris circa 1908 in aspic, were considered the height of modernity.

The situation did not change until these new ideas were brought to Britain by émigrés from the USSR (Berthold Lubetkin, Serge Chermayeff), Germany (Erich Mendelsohn, Walter Gropius, Moholy-Nagy), Austria (Ernst Freud), Czechoslovakia (Eugene Rosenberg) Finland (Cyril Mardall) or Hungary (Marcel Breuer, Ernő Goldfinger). Even those habitually classed as 'English' were actually colonials, such as the Japanese-Canadian Wells Coates, or New Zealanders Amyas Connell and

Basil Ward. From around 1933, these exiles began building in the European manner, usually private homes on the outskirts of London, eliciting the wrath of the RIBA president Reginald Blomfield, who attacked them in distinctly racialised terms as exponents of rootless, cosmopolitan 'Modernismus'. Pick admired this work, but was unwilling to follow it the whole way into white-walled abstraction and Year Zero techno-aesthetics.

Thus compromise was the watchword from the beginning. The major 1920s building commissioned by the Underground and designed by Charles Holden is the Underground Group (then the LPTB, then eventually TfL) headquarters, at 55 Broadway in St James, on top of the St James's Park underground station. Fifty-five Broadway, begun in 1926, is exactly contemporary with such fearless, uncompromising statements of modern architecture as the Bauhaus building in Dessau or the Gosprom building in Kharkiv. It is also contemporary with the style that actually dominated interwar Britain – the slightly naughtily unorthodox neo-baroque architecture of Edwin Lutyens, Herbert Baker, John Belcher or John Burnet. This was the architecture of the imperial twilight, alternately pompous and eyebrow-raisingly self-effacing, both a refusal to break in any way with the classical tradition and, often, an elaborate in-joke at its expense.

At 55 Broadway, a steel-framed tower of near-skyscraper dimensions is weighed down by heavy, non-structural Portland stone cladding, and the windows are of Georgian proportions. This 'compromise' is then offset by something quite fearless: the building is decorated with modernist sculpture. Some of it is subtly placed – statues of the 'winds' on the building's towering wings by Henry Moore, Eric Gill and Eric Aumonier – but some of it is outright confrontational, in the alternately elemental and overpowering, vital and gloomy, personifications of 'Night' and 'Day' by Jacob Epstein that mark the entrances to the Tube station underneath. In fact, in Rotterdam, Moscow or Berlin at that time the building would have seemed deeply conservative, but this didn't stop 55 Broadway, particularly its sculptures (one of which visibly had a penis), causing a minor moral panic in the tabloid press. Meanwhile, Piccadilly Circus was remodelled from the usual London chaos into a streamlined underground rotunda, lined in imperial travertine and equipped with the widest use of escalators in any public building up to that point – which featured, like most of Holden's stations, slightly pagan uplighters the length of the escalator.

Pick and Holden travelled around Europe in 1930 collecting ideas, and the results can be found up and down the Piccadilly Line. Scale and tiling is taken from Alfred Grenander's work on the Berlin U-Bahn, station infrastructure is taken from the newly built Hamburg Hochbahn, and much of the furniture and fittings (seats, signs, lamps, etc.) are borrowed from the Stockholm Expo of that year, which showcased a lighter, friendlier modernism than was the norm in the USSR or the Weimar Republic. The delicate yet laconic brickwork, which is usually considered to be the most 'Anglicised' part of the designs, is actually taken from the 'conservative modernist' work of the Dutch architect Willem Marinus Dudok. And that rotunda at

Arnos Grove draws on a similarly perfectly proportioned one by the unorthodox Swedish classicist Gunnar Asplund for the Stockholm Central Library, although it's hardly an imitation.

Everywhere, the harder meat of continental modernism – the increasingly all-glazed walls being used by functionalists in Germany or Czechoslovakia, the flying walkways and skyways of the Soviet constructivists, the pure white as-if-from-icing forms of Le Corbusier – is avoided in favour of something warmer and softer. This fits very closely with a certain form of English self-presentation in the interwar years. In Peter Mandler's words: 'Britain's avoidance of totalitarianism ... led to an orgy of anatomising, congratulating and self-congratulating on the English national character',[21] able to avoid all the extremes that those hysterical foreigners were indulging in. While Britain was patting itself on the back for moderation, it was of course expanding its empire across the Arabian peninsula, and gassing uppity natives in Mesopotamia.

In many cases, especially as the 1930s went on, this tamed modernism was combined with applied art that evoked the history of the areas into which the stations were built. For almost all of them, the underground was the force that actually helped them develop into suburbs. It was the planned, semi-socialist nationalised infrastructure that gave rise to unplanned speculative development, in the form of the endless mock-Tudor semis that spread across the London commuter belt frequently after, not before, a Tube station was built.

Michael Saler portrays Pick in the 1930s as a man wracked

with guilt and foreboding. He became one of the leading advocates of the Green Belt that Herbert Morrison's LCC drew around the capital in 1934, as if to constrain his own company's otherwise unstoppable spread. He eventually blamed the modern art and modern design he himself had popularised for what he perceived as a debasement of the moral and aesthetic sense. His notes for a lecture to a meeting of railway engineers in 1932 read as follows: 'Look to the future. Dark. Hordes of aeroplanes. Deluges of parachutes. A new migration of the peoples. The dark ages return. Another civilisation. All with the aid of locomotion'.[22]

Given the horrors that mechanisation and 'locomotion' were creating, it is unsurprising that Pick's project became ever more obviously an attempt to fuse modernity with a deep English nostalgia. The British Pavilion that he curated for the 1937 Paris Expo, celebrated as we've seen by Alexandra Harris, was one example of this. That sudden shift towards a reconciliation with tradition can also be detected in certain stations completed in the second half of the 1930s. The platforms of East Finchley, Pick's local station, boast impressive glazed staircases that appear to have been lifted lock, stock and barrel from the work of Walter Gropius, alongside a metal archer designed by Eric Aumonier in a cutesy, modernised gothic style, as if someone had leapt out of an early medieval illuminated manuscript and got himself cast in concrete. Something similar can be found at Uxbridge station, where one of Holden's most confident modernist structures, a sweeping concrete hangar, leads to a stiffly symmetrical, semi-classical street frontage, towards which you are ushered by mock-medieval stained glass representing the historic

East Finchley station

town of Uxbridge's coat of arms. Pick often claimed that the reason for his veering back towards some kind of tradition was the essential unsuitability of modernism for the English psyche; but it was perhaps also something he took from Soviet precedent. Curiously, like many of the figures we will meet here, the hostility to Communism – precisely one of the 'extremes' that good old England had managed to escape through its deployment of Common Sense – didn't preclude a degree of fascination and collaboration with the Soviet Union. Pick advised on the Moscow Metro, receiving the Order of Lenin for his efforts. One of Holden's last Tube stations, Gants Hill, built after Pick's death, was a literal tribute to the Soviet system, codenamed 'Moscow' when under construction: a great barrel-vaulted hall with classical uplighters, completely unique in London. This dalliance with the totalitarian style can be seen even more imposingly in a building with a Pick connection, but not for the LPTB – Senate House.

Essex Moscow: Gants Hill

Senate House, designed as part of a never-to-be-completed masterplan for the University of London, is all of the things that Holden's London Transport stations are not. Whereas these are images of a public bureaucracy that only the most hysterical, Ayn Randian libertarian could possibly be afraid of, Senate House has long inspired a delicate terror, or rather the theatrical mock-terror that middle-brow English intellectuals often affect when they come across a particularly stark piece of architecture. Designed immediately after the first run of post-European tour Tube stations, it is a mini-skyscraper built partly from load-bearing Portland stone, a remarkably expensive and ambitious choice, designed, quite literally, to last a thousand years. The great stone buttress that goes up the middle of the facade performs a functional role, making the tower somewhat heavy. The original plan commissioned by William Beveridge would have included several mini-towers and entailed the demolition of much of Georgian Bloomsbury, but even in its pared-down form, it's impressive. It is habitually described, like many of the more imposing buildings of the 1930s, as a putative 'Hitler's headquarters', but this has no basis in fact.[23]

If Senate House can't be Nazi, then maybe it can be Communist. The epithet 'Stalinist' is often applied to it; and there is certainly some similarity to the stepped profile of many Stalinist skyscrapers in the massing of its tower, as there is to the ceremonial passageways favoured by Albert Speer in its publicly accessible, imposing and moodily lit ground-floor lobby. But the real problem with Senate House is that it does not present an image of Englishness that is in any way ingratiating. The bright red brick of the tube stations meant that they slotted neatly into even the most mundane of suburban streets; the Georgian details and sculptures adorning 55 Broadway impelled identification. Here, though, we see an image of sheer power. We will turn to the organisation that used the tower later – but

Beveridge's Headquarters

first, what actually was the aesthetic of British power in this era? And does it have anything to do with the nostalgic-modernist object world we've discussed here?

The Bengal Famine Commemorative Tea Towel

The politics behind this movement was rather vague and woolly, pleasantly left-wing without being Bolshevik. It was the sort of arts-and-crafts-infused Fabian Socialism that scared nobody (even if Orwell found in it the germ of a Soviet fifth column). Most of those involved held to a politics roughly on a continuum, from the Keynesian wing of the Liberal Party, like William Beveridge, to the right of the Labour Party, like Herbert Morrison. However, their ideas were fundamentally connected with the swiftly-passed-over, not-to-be-mentioned fact of Britain's Empire, which reached its greatest expanse in the interwar years.

The conduit through which the practice of Empire inter-twined itself with the story of benevolent proto-socialist bureaucracy was an interwar body called the Empire Marketing Board. In this context we will also find in the ex-LCC leader and Festival sponsor Herbert Morrison — that 'good old 'Erb' who rehoused and educated thousands of Londoners to an unprecedentedly high standard — an unambiguously imperialistic, white-supremacist foreign secretary. This, rather than the allegedly totalitarian nature of good public transport and clear design, is the dark underside of austerity-nostalgia aesthetics. It is notable that the tea towels and mugs produced by that industry almost never feature the work made for the Empire Marketing

Board, unlike work by the exact same designers for London Transport or the 1951 Festival. Looking at the mission of the EMB, it is easy to see why.

The major project of interwar 'benevolent bureaucracy' was infused by a deep nostalgia, an exercise in pervasive national self-flattery; but in contrast to the present project of nostalgia, the 'nation' and its imperial periphery were then regarded as strongly and indelibly linked. The EMB was founded by the Tory government of Stanley Baldwin in 1926 to encourage and publicise a new protectionist policy in the British Empire, which was moving from its habitual insistence upon free trade towards what was called Imperial Preference. In short, the EMB's role was to convince consumers in Britain and its vast multi-continental Empire to buy Empire-made goods, which were not necessarily cheaper.

The board was placed under the authority of Stephen Tallents, a civil servant who had played some role in anti-Bolshevik insurgency during Britain's intervention in the Russian Civil War, even serving for a time as the governor of Riga, after a short-lived Latvian Soviet Republic was suppressed by British gunboats. However, as British imperial bureaucrats went, Tallents was exceptionally progressive, and assembled around him the likes of Frank Pick, who headed the EMB's poster division. The young left-wing filmmaker, critic and proponent of 'documentary' (a term he coined), John Grierson, launched its film unit.

The Empire Marketing Board's connection with the projects of the London Underground, the London County Council, the GPO, the Festival of Britain and the Ministry of Information was not merely a question of personnel. It reflected a major shift in the way the British Empire worked and thought of itself – not necessarily one that was any fairer to non-British imperial subjects, but one that chimed with the growing tendency to statism and protectionism that culminated in certain facets of the welfare state.

The EMB's creation was a major victory for a long-running movement called 'social imperialism', or, more technocratically, 'tariff reform'. This referred to changing customs laws so that Empire goods were taxed less than non-Empire, creating a single Imperial bloc on the world market. This movement sprang from the belief that the Empire should be turned from a cash cow with a vague ideology of racial supremacy attached, into a great and conscious ideological project which happened to be economically beneficial to the centre; for its proponents like Cecil Rhodes, this was a means to buying the allegiance of a potentially hostile working class to the British state.

The relevance of this to post-war Keynesian ideas is clear in statements such as that of Viscount Milner, one of the major campaigners for 'tariff reform':

> It is surely better to pay a little more for your goods, and keep thousands of people in productive work, than to pay a little less for your goods, and have ultimately to devote what you have saved in that way to the relief of pauperism due to the loss of employment.[24]

This was a 'public works' argument for a unified, protected imperial market. In order to sell this project to the public, Milner appealed to a new notion of the Empire: not as something British workers half-thought about, if at all, either when flag-waving in the event of a war or wondering where the cotton they were spinning in their factories came from, but instead as a 'great family'.[25] Here was a metaphor that had purchase: a vast, industrial unit of global exploitation and trade was reimagined on the domestic scale.

This also had some support on the left. The influential early English socialist and enthusiastic racist Robert Blatchford, editor of the widely read socialist paper *The Clarion*, used the same metaphor. Explaining his support for imperial conflicts (Blatchford supported both the Boer War and the First World War), he declared:

> I am a Socialist. I believe that the nation should be a family ... I ask my fellow citizens to lay aside their liberalism and their Toryism, and to deal with an Imperial danger as Britons ... Let us first make the family safe as a family, and then we can settle our domestic differences within the shelter of the family defences.[26]

His peculiar kind of socialist imperialism was based upon opposition to the 'puritan', 'priggish', and anti-war politics that were common to both the small British Marxist parties, like the Social Democratic Federation, and to the much larger Independent Labour Party. While many of their leaders, even the hardly consistently anti-imperialist Ramsay Macdonald, opposed World War I, Blatchford simply insisted 'When England is at war, I'm English. I have no politics and no Party. I am English.'[27]

These were not isolated voices in early twentieth-century Britain, but major figures, and their unstable and contradictory combination of social reform, unified and protectionist markets, state power, traditionalism and nationalist rhetoric became a major spur to the image-world of benevolent bureaucracy. Most of all, it bolstered that unavoidable image of the British or Imperial 'family'.

Baldwin's Tory governments were more dabblers in social imperialism than fully-fledged converts, as the influence of the City of London was too huge to seriously endanger Free Trade. The EMB was a compromise, an attempt to test out the possibilities of protectionism via a public relations campaign, rather than a total economic rebalancing.

The two major parts of the Empire Marketing Board for our purposes, the posters and the films, are of uneven importance. Frank Pick's stable of artists was directly redeployed from the Underground to the Empire. E. McKnight Kauffer's 1927 'Jungles Today Are Gold Mines Tomorrow' poster uses the same bright, jagged, slightly vorticist manner that induced commuters to go and live in Chingford. It features two African figures, one male and one female, the woman in a traditional head-dress holding aloft a pineapple, the man carrying a shield and staff; both have stylised features in a manner which now looks quite obviously racist.[28] In the imperial 'family', it is pretty clear that these are the children. Between the two bodies is a ship, and two columns of figures in pounds (received, sold, with the latter mostly higher), indicating the increase in trade between Britain and its African colonies between 1895 – around the time many of these colonies were acquired during the 'scramble for Africa' – and 1925.

This is an obvious image of plunder, belying the more high-minded intent that Pick had for the EMB. He insisted on greater artistic standards than was the norm for commercial posters, and took complete control over the selection of artists and designers, to devise a marketing plan whereby EMB publicity materials were deliberately placed separately from the main displays of shops and the main billboard locations. Posters were distributed to schools, and window displays were orchestrated to create what Pick called 'one vast Imperial advertisement'.[29]

Many of the posters offered a simple message, presented in the neat serif fonts recently used in World War I propaganda. The most straightforward series asks you to buy the products of various colonies and white-settler Dominions. 'BUY SOUTH AFRICAN ORANGES', over a painting of gazelles; 'BUY CANADIAN HAMS AND BACON', over one of a bison; and more strangely, 'BUY BRITISH WEST INDIAN ST VINCENT ARROWROOT' over an image of a turtle. Note that only the West Indies, a colony rather than a Dominion, needs to be specified as British.

Another campaign consists of two posters, 'EAST AFRICAN TRANSPORT OLD STYLE' and 'EAST AFRICAN TRANSPORT TODAY'. In 'old style', a group of Africans – again with those stylised, over-emphasised skulls, lips, noses and brows, painted so black they're almost purple – are marching with their livestock across the orange grass of a fauvist savannah. By contrast, 'today' shows those same East Africans trading with a benevolent white man, in a white shirt, who occupies high ground at the front of the scene. However creepy these images might be, there are several important points about them that should not be missed. Pick's selection and direction was intended to emphasise that on the one hand the Empire was, to use Ferdinand Tönnies' ever-useful distinction, a *Gesellschaft* – a modern network, linked by modern international transport, industry and communications. At the same time the posters also evoked a *Gemeinschaft*, a warm and inclusive family where everyone knows and works for and with each other, even the members of the family in faraway parts of the globe, who are raised to full 'adulthood' by the senior members of the network/family.

These images are now easily dismissed, and they have slipped almost entirely out of design history. The 'EMB' kitemark never became anywhere near as famous as the London Underground roundel. The project made little impact and was wound up in 1933, not so much because of protests – in the era of the Amritsar massacre and the pacification of Iraq, this was not a time when many people had qualms about repression, let alone objected to the benevolent exploitation depicted in EMB posters – but because it was considered a waste of money. The British consumers were found not to be particularly imperialist in their consumer choices.

If it is forgotten in poster or industrial design, the Empire Marketing Board is much more significant in the history of British cinema, for essentially being the first version of the team that would later produce the General Post Office Film Unit and the Ministry of Information's Crown Film Unit, that is, the partnership of the bureaucrat Stephen Tallents and the sociologist-critic-filmmaker John Grierson. Many of the works of the 'British Documentary Movement', such as Robert Flaherty's *Industrial Britain*, Basil Wright's *Song of Ceylon* and Grierson's own *Drifters*, were made for the Empire Marketing Board Film Unit. With startling naiveté for a man usually celebrated for his hard-headed realism, Grierson imagined that 'for the old flags of exploitation, (the EMB) substitutes the new flags of common labour'.[30] This social imperialism was shared by Tallents, who had a remarkably avant-garde conception of the means for propagandising it, pungently described by historian Scott Anthony as 'a mix of cutting-edge nostalgia, rustic sci-fi and neo-Soviet bombast'.[31]

Stephen Tallents's ideas on propaganda and public relations were the result of two unusual experiences for a British civil servant. In Estonia and in Latvia, as governor of Riga, Tallents was able to observe first-hand a complex, multifaceted conflict between imperial interests (German Freikorps, British gunboats and White Russian generals squabbling over the Baltic) and revolution, as relentless Bolshevik and Spartacist propaganda appealed with considerable success to proletarian soldiers who, the line went, 'had no country'. A more prosaic spell working as an administrator of labour exchanges (early Job Centres) had convinced him that existing civil service practice was not only inefficient, but deeply humiliating towards the working-class users of the interwar years' skeletal welfare system.

Accordingly, Tallents's conception of PR and propaganda seems remarkably humane and democratic, especially when compared with the brute cynicism of American contemporaries such as Edward Bernays. His biographer Scott

Anthony cites his statement of intent: public relations must lead 'the public to take the most economic advantages of the facilities which they have caused to be provided for themselves'.[32] There could be no better short description of the project of benevolent bureaucracy. Similarly, Tallents was in no doubt that in the Empire 'human life and health were being wasted on a gigantic scale'. However, he imagined that an imperial problem could be solved by imperial methods, by encouraging 'imperial development' rather than raw exploitation.[33]

His approach to this rebranded empire was deeply influenced by another, much more convincingly rebranded empire – the transformation of the Russian Empire, consisting of a large chunk of eastern Europe, 'all the Russias', the Caucasus and 'Turkestan', into the Union of Soviet Socialist Republics, a putative union of disparate sovereign states that specified no ruling nation or even geographical region. This was something that was perhaps honoured mostly in the breach, but it remained Tallents's great exemplar. His interest was in Soviet propaganda, and most of all, Soviet film.

Given that this is around the time that 'Bolshie' entered the lexicon as an insult, and given that the entire English self-image was based upon not being totalitarian Europeans, and given that Soviet films were routinely banned, this was a daring direction indeed. Tallents propounded his ideas in a 1932 pamphlet, *The Projection of England*, which is often seen as prefiguring the more famous work of the GPO Film Unit, but which could equally easily be seen as a statement of intent for the Empire Marketing Board. This is not as strange as it may appear. Of the Soviet films Tallents cited – *Battleship Potemkin*, Oleksandr Dovzhenko's *Earth*, Viktor Turin's *Turksib*, and Vsevolod Pudovkin's *Storm over Asia* – not one is set in Russia itself (and only one was directed by an 'ethnic Russian'). These films showed, according to Tallents, what 'an incomparable instrument for national expression the cinema might be'.[34] Accordingly, they proved to be useful models for the projection of England into that imperial space defined by the EMB.

This is classic British rhetoric – *they* disguise their aesthetic intent in order to make propaganda, while what the Empire Marketing Board did was selflessly display the beauty of South African countryside, or inform buyers of ham in Luton or tyres in Gosforth that it would be better if they bought it from the Empire.

The two most enduring of the EMB's films are Wright's *Song of Ceylon*, actually released in 1934 just after the EMB's dissolution, and Flaherty's *Industrial Britain* (1931). On an artistic level, *Song of Ceylon* is far superior to what would be expected of a propaganda film for the British Empire. With its pulsating, woozy music, images of ritual dances, and atmosphere of the past in the present, it is intense and heady. It shifts constantly from sociology or generalisation – for the Sinhalese, say, 'to work for hire is a great shame, and there are very few here that will work so' – through a constructivist-style depiction of the beauty of labour to an attempt at a filmic representation of the impersonal forces of globalisation. In the film's third part, a voice from nowhere promises to these rural labourers a world of new technologies, new communications, 'new development of national resources', over images of a man riding an elephant.

You gradually realise these voices are connected with the trading of Ceylon's tea, and its position on the stock market, as you now watch men walk barefoot in the forest. You realise these two things are directly connected. A crescendo of radio crackle accompanies these men and women bending over to pick tea. Then you see the tea being processed. Torqued just a little, you could imagine this as a critique of the way these people are exploited – we certainly do not see them benefitting from the fruits of their labours being sold off and distributed around Europe. What we do sense is that it doesn't really matter, because this is the way these people have lived, and the way they will always live.

Robert Flaherty's *Industrial Britain*, meanwhile, is the product not of a left-leaning London intellectual, but, at least in part, of an American director better known for man-versus-nature works such as *Nanook of the North* and *Man of Aran*. The heroic narration (imposed by Grierson) often seems at odds with Flaherty's careful, sensitive depiction of the intricate processes of work in potteries, mines, glass furnaces and so forth. 'The industrial towns are not quite so drab as they seem – behind their smoke, beautiful things are being made!' booms the voiceover, and as much as any Vertov, Flaherty was capable of filming the beauty of steelworks, smoking chimneys and spindly gantries. Eventually, however, the lack of any sense that we're dealing with a society rather than a few individual labourers makes *Industrial Britain* as much of a tribute to lone men against nature as any of Flaherty's better known documentaries.

Both *Song of Ceylon* and *Industrial Britain* manage to be formally radical and deeply, poignantly beautiful, while giving the impression that their protagonists are just fine with their place in the world.

Although *Song of Ceylon* has a wide reputation, it is notable that the 'British documentary movement', though it grew out of an institution designed to rebrand and recharge the Empire, is way better known for its films about Britain than for those on Sri Lanka or the Caribbean. This is partly due to the fact that shortly after its dissolution, the Empire Marketing Board Film Unit was transformed into the General Post Office Film Unit, with practically the same staff – John Grierson, Basil Wright, Alberto Cavalcanti, under the generous yet watchful eye of Sir Stephen Tallents.

The GPO Film Unit, like the London Passenger Transport Board, can be credited with a remarkable dissemination of avant-garde work to a public that is generally assumed to be hostile to any kind of experimentation. If anything the GPO Unit was even more radical than London Transport, keener to promote the genuine cutting edge of the period. Its short animated and montage films, especially – distributed as packages, to be shown before main features, but also circulated in schools and film clubs – are remarkably ebullient, bright, all-gates-open documents of filmic possibility.

The most recognisable example of the British documentary movement is Basil Wright and Harry Watt's *Night Mail*, released in 1936, a night in the life of the Postal Special on its way from London to the cities of Scotland. Speaking later of the GPO Film Unit's portrayal of the working class – by then being presented by earnestly anachronistic scholars as 'paternalist' – Alberto Cavalcanti fairly pointed out that 'workers previously in film had been a kind of comical relief. Since the documentary they became part of humanity.'[35] These workers are not anonymous components of a collective instrument bent on transforming the world, they are fag-smoking, beer-drinking, flirtatious men (usually men) who work hard but would probably rather be putting their feet up with a cuppa – the 'inherently decent' British prole idealised and objectified by George Orwell as a fundamentally stupid but noble animal, in whom 'hope' may or may not lie. As Scott Anthony puts it, 'there isn't any dialogue in Dziga Vertov that sees the proletarian exclamation "Take it away, sonny boy!" answered with a chirpy "Right-ho, handsome!"'[36] This is quite some improvement on either their depiction as comic foils in the 1930s, or as grunting TV-addicted lumpen in the twenty-first century. The 'Guild Socialists' of the railway workers' union were firm supporters of the GPO Film Unit's activities, so it's no surprise that at the start of the film, 'The workers of the railway' are credited just after Wright, Watt and Cavalcanti. Not credited are the film's most famous contributors, composer Benjamin Britten and, writing the closing verses that are the film's most instantly quotable moment, W. H. Auden.

If this documentary movement is a 'projection of England', it is done with a sureness, egalitarianism, humour and visual flair that equal its inadvertent Soviet tutors. It offers a vision of England that strives to include everything and everyone.

Except, of course, Britain's Empire.

Given the Film Unit's new function as the propaganda service for a rather less controversial institution, there might appear to be little thematic overlap. There is just one exception – an entirely forgotten 1938 film called *God's Chillun*, with the telling working title of 'Negroes'. Here, many of the protagonists of *Night Mail* reprise their roles. The music is again by Benjamin Britten, there are verses by W. H. Auden, and the footage was collected by Basil Wright on an Empire Marketing Board-funded trip to the 'British West Indies' in 1933.

Unlike the average EMB poster display, *God's Chillun* is not easily taken as a work of unambiguous imperial propaganda, and unlike *Song of Ceylon*, it tries to criticise certain aspects of British imperialism. It's close to the impossible anti-imperialist imperialism that John Grierson wanted to make out of the EMB Film Unit. It begins with sixteenth-century images of the New World, telling us of the various peoples that now live there; then the film switches into a precise description of the extermination of the natives, and mentions 'the slave ships that surrounded the mouth of every river'. We are shown the notorious sketch-plans of those ships, with the voices alternating from RP to a Caribbean accent, and 'slave songs' written by Auden sounding in the background.

Wright's 1933 footage is of black bodies engaged in hard, agricultural, physical labour, and though the historic images montaged into it tell us how good the 'advanced European thinkers' were for setting these people free in the nineteenth century, the harshness of the footage tells its own story. The directors then, as if worried they'd gone too far, give the last word to a white, Cambridge-educated West Indies cricketer, who assures us that things might be bad, but with the Empire's help are getting better, particularly since the advent of compulsory primary education. 'The light', the voiceover intones, 'falls equally on black and white'.

It is easy to see why something like *God's Chillun* has sunk almost without trace, while *Night Mail* has become a modern classic, and it's not only because the old habit of pretending the Empire didn't exist has now become a similar habit of pretending it never happened. But here the compromise goes so far as to make any argument incomprehensible and incoherent, straining against impossible limits. When it came to the Empire, one could not be socialist and imperialist, egalitarian and paternalist, without collapsing into a mess of picturesque platitudes.

Socialists like Grierson, and social democrats like Frank Pick, tried with some seriousness to represent the British Empire as part of the British 'family' they imagined. For them it was important to stress the potential benefits of, say, radio and mass production to the people of Ceylon or Jamaica, much as they propagandised the way the post and the tube civilised and united London. The brutality and sheer scale of exploitation at the heart of the Empire necessarily made that a somewhat grotesque juxtaposition. It seems therefore all the more curious that the austerity-nostalgia imaginary should be so ruthlessly scrubbed of any connection to the Empire, not only of its existence and aesthetics during the period being remembered and referenced, but also in terms of any cultural or political input whatsoever into British culture from the descendants of those migrants who came from the Empire's peripheries. The world of Hauntology, as much as the world of *Romantic Moderns*, is one where Britain never faced mass migration, and our music and culture never absorbed the internationalisation, Americanisation and de-Europeanisation that came with it. As much as austerity nostalgia is the imaginary vision of a Britain without 1979 and Thatcher, it's also a Britain without 1948 and the Empire Windrush.

4

Family Portrait

I am not a Communist, I am a Social Democrat. I believe that it is possible for a modern intelligent community to organise its economic life rationally, with decent orders of priority, and it is not necessary to resort to a dictatorship in order to do it. I believe that it is possible. That is why I am a Socialist. If I did not believe that, I would be a Communist. I would not be a capitalist! I believe that this country of ours and this movement of ours, despite our setbacks, nevertheless is being looked upon by the rest of the world as the custodian of democratic representative government. But, comrades, if we are going to be a custodian, we must at the same time realise what the job is. The job is that we must try and organise our economic life intelligently and rationally in accordance with some order of priorities and a representative government ... In modern complex society it is impossible to get rational order by leaving things to private economic adventure. Therefore I am a Socialist.

Aneurin Bevan, speech to the Labour Party Conference, 1959[1]

'I Suppose We Have to Carry On, But ...'

The 1940s, first the 'People's War' and then the apparent social revolution of 1945–51, is the common fixation for all varieties of austerity nostalgia, uniting left and right, aesthetes and cooks, politicians and art historians. Accordingly, it's worth looking at some of the obsessed-over moments in a little more detail, to check the hazy romantic picture against the historical record. One useful source for this is another institution of the post-war period that warms the cockles of austerity nostalgics: Mass Observation. Including in its ranks surrealists and aesthetes like Humphrey Jennings, this organisation attempted to create a sort of archaeology of the present, periodically presenting its findings to government as a way of inducing them to pursue less elitist policies. MO is largely remembered today for its influence on what would later become market research, but its archives have also produced several intriguing books on the era which run strikingly counter to the accepted narrative. Easy distinctions between political movements in the original austerity era are hard to ratify in the various diaries collected in Simon Garfield's *Our Hidden Lives*, where we find a Workers Educational Association member glumly voting Tory and bickering in empty rooms over historical minutiae, a barely closeted gay Edinburgh antique dealer, and a Labour-voting, socialist Sheffield housewife confiding to her diary that she understands why Hitler wanted to get rid of the Jews.

In particular, *Living through the Blitz*, edited by MO's Tom Harrisson, makes clear just how much the '1945' we now consume is a construct, a convenient fairy tale built up piece by piece several generations later. Most interesting for our purposes is its plentiful evidence that the imperative (in rhetoric, if not in the specific form of the unprinted poster) to 'Keep Calm and Carry On' actually had much the opposite effect. The patronising message infuriated most of the scores of mostly working-class diarists and interviewees whose materials make up the book. And rather than an alliance between the 'decent' people and their 'decent', benevolent public servants, *Living through the Blitz* finds a total divorce between the interests of each, with the civil service and local government desperately scared of the workers they were supposed to be sheltering from bombs.

For example, while the Labour left and radical architects were advocating communal shelters, central government had a firm preference for the privatisation of bomb protection. 'Whitehall', Harrisson writes, 'had long declared that there must be no "shelter mentality". If big, safe, deep shelters were established, people would simply lie in them and do no work. Worse, such concentrations of proletarians could be breeding grounds for mass hysteria, even subversion. The answer was the Anderson shelter.'[2] That is, private shelters in back gardens, not necessarily safer, but less likely to encourage sedition.

The only major exception to this was the London Underground, which was first squatted at night against the LPTB's resistance, rather than at the benevolent behest of Pick and Ashfield, after which its use as a refuge was tacitly accepted. The picture of life in such public shelters as were built comes off as very different to the jolly calm knees-up we have been led to imagine. 'Here the ARP helper tries

once again to start some singing', writes one diarist. "Roll
out the …", she begins. "Shut your bleedin' row!" shouts a
woman of fifty. "We got enough noise without you.""[3]

In certain cities, this disjunction between the people and
their government nearly led to open revolt. Southampton,
for instance, was so heavily bombed in 1940 that many
refugees spread out in an arc across the surrounding
countryside, to Eastleigh, Chandlers Ford, Otterborne,
Twyford, Shawford, Winchester, Romsey, New Forest,
leaving a small and badly sheltered working-class population, who didn't have relatives to stay with, to bear the
brunt. The city council's leaders were among those that
departed, leading to an RAF coup in the city, where for a
time the city was run as a military dictatorship, with the
hapless civilian leadership in hiding. 'The airmen deeply
criticised the breakdown', writes Harrisson. 'They were
scathing about the leadership of the city as a whole', who
had 'quit intellectually, some of them actually, physically'.[4]

Mass Observation compiled a report in 1940 about the
reactions to the bombing of Southampton, and found that
'over and over again … homeless, old, pregnant, ill and
anxious-to-evacuate people … did not know where to
get the relevant forms or information. The comment of
one woman is not typical, but not too far away from it.
"Everywhere you go they tell you you can't go there.""[5]
On George VI's visit to the city, intended as a way of cheer-
ing up the battered populace, 'the party passed unnoticed.
When a large public later learned of their visitors, initially
from the radio, the response was far from uniformly enthusiastic … "I suppose they do a certain amount of good

coming around but I wish they'd give me a new house" [was] among the more friendly comments'.[6] Or, as another put it more bluntly, 'everybody knew [the council] got out of Southampton every night and only came back to meet the King and Queen'.[7]

Similar scenes in Liverpool led to a fear of riots or even insurrection. Here,

> there appeared by this time to be an 'almost complete divorce' between a few key politicians and officers at the top and the worried, bewildered 99 percent, with no serious attempt to keep the 99 percent informed about either present actions or future intentions. However impossible the situation, this total failure to communicate, this silence, seemed inexplicable. Nevertheless, rumour had it that the city's marble halls echoed with talk of 'honours', OBEs.[8]

One reaction to the Blitz was not so much anger as relief, in the dual sense of relief from an all-pervasive boredom as well as from danger. One diarist 'kept on saying to myself, over and over again, trying the phrase on, like a new dress, to see how it fitted: "I've been *bombed*!" "*I've* been bombed! – *Me*!" It seems a terrible thing to say, when so many people must have been killed and injured last night, but never in my life have I experienced such *pure and flawless happiness*.'[9] Or, similarly, another claimed 'I wouldn't mind having an evening like it say once a week. Ordinarily, there's no excitement, nothing to do or anything.'[10]

The Mass Observation reports on the Blitz urged the government – and, specifically, the Ministry of Information – to realise that the people being bombed were neither

restive Morlocks nor jolly Cockneys, but adult human
beings who appreciated neither being bombed nor being
patronised. 'You will hear a lot of talk', wrote one female
clerk and MO diarist from Manchester, 'about Manchester
carrying on. I suppose we are ... but as one who lives here,
it's a rather heavy carrying on. We are carrying on *because
we've got to*.'[11]

According to Harrisson,

> Those concerned with guiding the public mood, mostly through
> the Ministry of Information, for a long time took a contrary view.
> They urged 'YOUR COURAGE, YOUR CHEERFULNESS,
> YOUR RESOLUTION, WILL BRING US VICTORY' in a
> poster which exactly defined the distinction between the Minister
> (we) and the Mass (you).

After the infuriated reaction that this elicited, and after
the feared mass panics and riots didn't occur, 'instruc-
tions to the Assistance Board, for instance, "began to be
coloured with significant references to the need for cour-
teous and sympathetic behaviour". They had not been
there before.'[12]

The picture of all those interwar institutions that
emerges here chimes with the austerity discourse that we
hear today. They appear not as modernising or benevolent,
but as brutally, ignorantly Victorian. 'The poor, the homeless and the deprived, were on no account to be encouraged
to sponge on society. The Blitz made misfortune and depri-
vation indiscriminate, unearned. But the organisation and
routine of public assistance was ill-designed for dealing

with situations requiring generosity, sympathy and spontaneity.'[13] The reality of 1945 was not a continuation of the public culture of the interwar years, but – for the millions of working-class people who voted for serious and lasting social change – a rejection of institutions that had treated them like scum, unless they were lucky enough to be considered 'deserving'. A Blitzed docker from Southampton or millworker from Manchester, transplanted from 1940 to 2015 to see posters everywhere telling them to 'Keep Calm and Carry On', would, aside from being puzzled by a poster they'd never seen before, have recognised that something they had actually fought against was being reproduced as a nightmarish farce, a carrying on not 'because we have to' – because the alternative is Nazism – but out of a perverse lifestyle choice, and as a consequence of an economic dogma they had struggled bloody hard to destroy. So, if the mythology of the classless 'Blitz spirit' is so spurious, how might other myths of austerity hold up – those of George Orwell, or the Attlee government, for instance?

Listening to Britain

However much those actually bombed were angered by the patronising posters and the inefficient, cowardly public administration, it won't do to argue that all of the wartime propaganda effort was on this level. The more radical ideas of the 1930s bureaucracies did have some role. In 1939, the GPO Film Unit was rebranded and dedicated to a different public institution, the Ministry of Information, as the Crown Film Unit, with most of the same protagonists in place. However, the great films of the Crown Film Unit are not whimsical avant-garde shorts or neo-Soviet celebrations of industry, but a series of moving war-propaganda films by the surrealist and minor GPO director, Humphrey Jennings. Here, even the English eye most inclined to resist the call of 'progressive patriotism' succumbs to the portrayal of England as this idealised, egalitarian family. Films such as *Fires Were Started*, or the dialogue and narration-free *Listen to Britain* (1942) are unbearably sad and humane.

Listen to Britain is a matter of montage, juxtapositions, poetic and associative. Planes, fields, silhouettes watching the sea, then putting their helmets on; a slow dance, roll out the barrel; the chug of trains, clanking of the aircraft hangar and the buzz of a warplane; then a recital, a horse-drawn cart in front of smoking chimneys, the panorama of an industrial city. A train slides past Battersea Power Station. Children playing. Armoured cars rolling through country villages. A radio shouts 'Calling all workers!' and a car veers towards a railway bridge across which rushes a smoking locomotive. Now it's 'workers' playtime' at a munitions factory full of women, who absentmindedly sing and dance along to a tango. Music-hall singers and noted anti-fascists Flanagan and Allen sway dryly from side to side, their voices echoing around a huge assembly of workers.[14] National Gallery. The Queen Mum watches the pianist Myra Hess play Beethoven. The reactions of onlookers – moved, but not hysterical. Everything comes to a crescendo, with ports, industry, tanks, parades through a town, rippling crops, cooling towers, parting clouds and the sound of 'Rule Britannia'.

Jennings's last film, *Family Portrait*, a summation of British technological and sociological achievement that exudes a strangely melancholic air, was made for the Lion and the Unicorn Pavilion – Stephen Tallents's main contribution to the Festival of Britain in 1951, curated to explore 'British identity'. Both this vision of a populist, decent, essentially sort-of-socialist Britain and the pavilion's name itself evokes a writer who is the forefather of all Progressive Patriots: the India-born, Eton-educated former Burmese policeman, Eric Arthur Blair, aka George Orwell. His 1940 pamphlet *The Lion and the Unicorn: Socialism and the English Genius* was not particularly widely read at the time, the left-wing mood of the troops being shaped much more by passed-around copies of J. B. Priestley's *English Journey* and Robert Tressell's *The Ragged-Trousered Philanthropists*; but it has dominated much of the subsequent discussion.

In the hindsight of twenty-first-century editorialists, it was Orwell who, unbeknownst to the public, captured the mood that would lead from the 'People's war' through to the establishment of the welfare state and the Cold War. Considering that his fame during his lifetime was owed to his late-career anti-communist satires rather than his work on English identity, Orwell is a fitting figure for our contemporary 'Legislated Nostalgia'. *The Lion and the Unicorn* is also responsible for one of the most influential conceptions of Britain as a 'family', a metaphor that, as we've seen, stretches from the 'social imperialists' or the Empire Marketing Board's notion of an imperial family, to the cosy home economics of David Cameron and George Osborne, where the British household, having 'maxed out its credit card', was 'all in this together', scrimping and saving to pay it off. Orwell, having seen, participated in, and been horrified by the brutalities of imperialism, was not so foolish as to argue that the Empire was a family of any kind. He purposefully restricted the metaphor to Britain, and added the all-important proviso that it was 'a family with the wrong members in control'; a country run by the 'old and silly'.[15]

Orwell did have a strong idea of who was the cuckoo in the family's nest: left-wing intellectuals. These deracinated pen-pushers might have tried to deny it or replace it, but the fact was,

> one cannot see the modern world as it is unless one recognises the overwhelming strength of patriotism, of national loyalty. In certain circumstances it can break down, at certain levels of civilisation it does not exist, but as a *positive* force there is nothing to set beside it. Christianity and international Socialism are as weak as straw in comparison with it.[16]

For the true, free-born Englishman, the nation is eternal, and can be summed up by a list that Orwell expected the average 1940s reader to find instantly, poignantly evocative: 'the clutter of clogs in the Lancashire mill-towns, the to-and-fro of lorries on the Great North Road, the queues around the Labour Exchanges, the rattle of pintables in the Soho pubs, the old maids biking to Holy Communion through the mists of the autumn morning'. However much the more extreme factions of austerity-nostalgics might try to revive it, and retailers of austerity-look stuff like Labour and Wait might try to provide it, the fact is that, aside from 'the queues round the Labour Exchanges' – or rather, in a grammatical mangling that would have mortified but vindicated Orwell, around the Newspeak-esque Jobcentre Plus – absolutely none of this exists.

The Great North Road is now the M1, where lorries toing-and-froing would fall foul of speed cameras. Clogs are not worn in the mill-less Lancashire towns. Those devout cycling old maids may be limited to the furthest backwaters of rural England, except perhaps if they're cycling to West African evangelical churches. Even Jamie Oliver's Ministry of Food daren't reintroduce the once-ubiquitous suet dumpling. When John Major adapted the list in the early 1990s, adding still-extant phenomena such as warm beer, cricket and 'invincible' suburbs, he dropped many of Orwell's specifics, knowing they had disappeared. Orwell had, details aside, described the 'structure of feeling' later evoked in the 1980s and 1990s by John Major, The Smiths or Billy Bragg, and debased more recently by Jon Cruddas or Mumford & Sons.

The Lion and the Unicorn was also Orwell's nearest approach to a political programme, and here, the former Burmese policeman's attitude towards the Empire is interesting, shifting so quickly from one perspective to another that you might accuse him of Doublethink. Even at his most flag-waving, Orwell insists that 'the standard of living of the trade-union workers, whom the Labour Party represents, depends indirectly on the sweating of Indian coolies',[17] and proposes a Commonwealth be created out of the Empire. This is not independence as we know it, but a sort of a socialist federation, taking into account that 'in

the age of the tank and the bombing plane, backward agricultural countries like India and the African colonies can no
more be independent than can a cat or a dog.'[18]

Here, the Imperial family is too human, and has become
instead the Imperial menagerie. However, as a recently
escaped veteran of Spain's persecuted Partido Obrero de
Unificación Marxista and active member of the Independent
Labour Party, Orwell's first response to the war and its
pretensions was total revulsion. On the eve of the war,
in the tactfully titled 1939 essay 'Not Counting Niggers',
Orwell analyses a proposal that the 'democracies' – at that
point, Britain, France, the Low Countries, Scandinavia
and Czechoslovakia – unite into a federal super-state to
counter the Third Reich. Such proposals 'coolly lump the
huge British and French empires – in essence nothing but
mechanisms for exploiting cheap coloured labour – under
the heading of democracies!'

This habit of thought, where liberal democracy's illib-
eral and undemocratic relationship to the rest of the planet
is ignored, has persisted long since, especially among the
keepers of the Orwell legacy. Orwell himself was merciless
in exposing it:

Here and there ... though not often, there are references to the
'dependencies' of the democratic states. 'Dependencies' means
subject races ... The unspoken clause is always 'not counting
niggers'. For how can we make a 'firm stand' against Hitler if
we are simultaneously weakening ourselves at home? In other
words, how can we 'fight Fascism' except by bolstering up a far
vaster injustice? For of course it *is* vaster. What we always forget

is that the overwhelming bulk of the British proletariat does not live in Britain, but in Asia and Africa. It is not in Hitler's power, for instance, to make a penny an hour a normal industrial wage; it is perfectly normal in India, and we are at great pains to keep it so. One gets some idea of the real relationship of England and India when one reflects that the *per capita* annual income in England is something over £80, and in India about £7. It is quite common for an Indian coolie's leg to be thinner than the average Englishman's arm. And there is nothing racial in this, for well-fed members of the same races are of normal physique; it is due to simple starvation. This is the system which we all live on and which we denounce when there seems to be no danger of its being altered. Of late, however, it has become the first duty of a 'good anti-Fascist' to lie about it and help to keep it in being.[19]

Although it would be overtaken by events (the Third Reich's ghettos, prisoner of war camps and death camps would soon surpass the British Empire's moral depths), this is the sort of rhetoric which Orwell's contemporary followers would ridicule as 'relativism' or 'whataboutery'. The Empire Marketing Board and its social-imperialist ilk have little place here.

So what happened? How did we get from here to the prospect of the British family keeping and tending its Indian and African cats and dogs? In Orwell's remarkably candid, but unmistakeably bizarre personal account, he had a dream on the eve of the war in which Britain was under attack. At that point he instantly switched to Progressive Patriotism, and started accusing pacifists of being 'objectively pro-Hitler'. This moment of revelation is often presented as deeply sincere and honest, which it was, but it is also so personal a reaction, and so narrowly middle-class, that it's strange to universalise it. 'It was one of those dreams which, whatever Freudian inner meaning they may have, do sometimes reveal to you the real state of your feelings.' He argues, convincingly, that it is a nonsense to fight fascism in Spain and then refuse to fight Hitler, just because the British Army is doing so. But then he admits that this is merely a post-facto rationalisation: 'what I knew in my dream that night was that the long drilling in patriotism which the middle classes go through had done its work, and that once England was in a serious jam it would be impossible for me to sabotage. But let no-one mistake the meaning of this. Patriotism has nothing to do with conservatism.'[20] An argument is made which the author tells you quite plainly is irrational, only to proceed to make a rational case for it – pouring scorn on the usual enemy, i.e. pansy left-wing intellectuals, for the fact that they are incapable of understanding it. Cosmopolitans unbellyfeel Ingsoc.

In 1947, Orwell wrote an essay called 'Towards European Unity' in which he proposed the creation of a remarkably similar Northern-European bloc (this time to fight for democratic socialism against the Americans and the Soviets) to the one he had rhetorically annihilated in 1939. His rationale is that this area – roughly a quadrilateral with, at its corners, Finland, Ireland, France and Italy – is the only area to keep alive any notion of socialism, especially given that 'the Asiatic nationalist movements are either Fascist in character, or look towards Moscow [or] are tinged by racial mysticism.'[21] Somehow, this is to be reconciled with a serious transformation of the Empire, and that, specifically, might be its undoing, for Orwell has not forgotten that

> the European peoples, and especially the British, have long owed their high standard of life to direct or indirect exploitation of the coloured peoples. This relationship has never been made clear by official socialist propaganda, and the British worker, instead of being told that by world standards, he is living above his income, has been taught to think of himself as an overworked, down-trodden slave.

A viable democratic socialism, for Orwell, simply *must* mean a poorer West and a richer South. 'Morocco or Nigeria or Abyssinia must cease to be colonies and instead become autonomous republics on a complete equality with the European peoples.' This would very probably make British workers poorer, and 'if he has been taught to see socialism in materialistic terms', the worker might reject an impoverished, if independent socialism and 'decide it is better to remain an imperial power at the expense of playing second fiddle to America'.

This makes striking reading alongside the Blue Labour tendency to back up the prejudices of those workers fearful of their status being undermined by foreigners. For Orwell, any socialism worthy of the name (which, for him, the Soviet Union certainly wasn't) must almost inevitably see the living standards of the British worker be undermined in the interest of foreigners. For all of Orwell's occasionally creepy generalisations, this is a statement far too radical in its implications to be countenanced – the maintenance of severe austerity throughout Europe as a means of improving the lot of the exploited peoples of Asia and Africa.

Orwell's idea of austerity is, then, a deeply unusual one; but that doesn't exhaust the connections between the great man and the 1940s moment of restricted consumption and total mobilisation. Reading *Nineteen Eighty-Four* through the cabbage-steam and Bovril fug of austerity nostalgia, it is unavoidable how much of it is suffused with the atmosphere of austerity – its iconography, its buildings, its jobs. Winston Smith works for the Ministry of Truth (a stand-in for the Ministry of Information), which is housed in something closely resembling the hulk of Senate House towering over the grimy squares of North London, 'startlingly different from any other object in sight ... an enormous pyramidal structure of glittering white concrete, soaring up, terrace after terrace'.[22] He learns and writes in Newspeak, a Stalinist version of the Basic English devised in the 1930s by Ogden and Richards, the rights to which were bought by the British government. He lives in Victory Mansions, an unrenovated 1930s apartment block, all uneasy conversations on seedy stairwells, and he dreams of the 'golden country', a rural England of rolling fields and bright colours suffused in a charming haze – a vision which appears to owe more to one of E. McKnight Kauffer's fauvist posters imploring the London Underground commuter to visit Surrey or Berkshire than any actually experienced countryside. He drinks bad gin in dilapidated caffs, and dreams of real things like real coffee and real, easy women wearing real lipstick.

In *1984*, Michael Radford's film version of the book, the 1980s are rendered as a post-apocalyptic '40s, with cutglass, RP announcers, bad teeth, varicose veins, pervasive fogs and ubiquitous greys, browns and blues, twentiethcentury hell rendered as a bleak Sunday in Archway. Aside from Radford's remarkable, proto-austerity-nostalgic film, Anthony Burgess's 1978 essay *1985* is one of the few discussions to have captured the fact that *Nineteen Eighty-Four* is a book about post-war austerity as much, if not more, than it is a book about Stalinism or the Third Reich. Attempting to convince a sceptical interlocutor that Airstrip One in 1984 is really a transmutation of London in 1948, Burgess recalls those days: 'We had worse privations than during the war, and they seemed to get worse every week. The meat ration was down to a couple of slices of fatty corned beef. One egg a month, and the egg was usually bad. I seem to remember you could still get cabbages easily enough. Boiled cabbage was a redolent staple of the British diet ... You saw the effects of German bombing everywhere, with London pride and loosestrife growing brilliantly in the corners. It's all in Orwell.'[23] Not in Orwell, but equally redolent of this trend, were the post-war camps of Billy Butlin, a sort of totalitarianism without the terror, with 'a great deal of the army about it – reveille, cookhouses, dining-halls, organised diversions, physical jerks'.

Burgess would not live to see the fans of indie rock flock to Camber Sands to enjoy the same experience as a nostalgic treat.

In *The Lion and the Unicorn*, Orwell hopes that 1940 is the overture to the English Revolution, which will set up a Cheka, nationalise land and crush resistance, but keep the judges' wigs and the royal family intact. By 1948 he was disillusioned by the timidity of the Labour government, and concentrated instead on Ingsoc, where the *New Statesman* takes power and remakes Britain in its own image. Burgess, however, remembers 'English Socialism coming to power in 1945 ... they sang The Red Flag at the opening session of Parliament, it drowned God Save the King and Rule Britannia and Land of Hope and Glory'.[24] This was because the war really did have the radicalising effect that Orwell imputed to it. 'If a man entered the army as a mild radical,' Burgess writes, 'he approached the 1945 election as a raging one. A Welsh Sargeant summed it up to me. "When I joined up, I was red. Now I'm bloody purple." If the British Communist Party had fielded more candidates, the make-up of the first post-war British Parliament might have been very interesting indeed.'[25]

Rather tellingly, Burgess then goes on to explain that one of the main irritants for working-class soldiers and civilians, that sent them out to vote Labour in droves (even the Catholic conservative Burgess did so, for the first and last time in his life), was the 'posters put out by the Ministry of Information, mostly ham-handed, not subtly ambiguous like the Ingsoc ones.' They were instead patrician, lofty, and insulting: 'YOUR FORTITUDE, YOUR PATIENCE, YOUR ENDURANCE WILL BRING US VICTORY. You and us, you see. No wonder we all became bloody purple.'[26] This poster is, you'll notice, a slightly misremembered version of the slogan which was originally supposed, along with 'FREEDOM IS IN PERIL', to hang alongside

'KEEP CALM AND CARRY ON'. One can assume that if it had actually been used, it would have had an equally infuriating effect.

We can see that Orwell's 'austerity', at any rate, is not ours, and to blame him for the aesthetics of austerity nostalgia would be unfair. Is the claiming of him by Blue Labour and Red Toryism as the prophet of Progressive Patriotism any more accurate? Orwell's ideas about the working class weren't that far from the currently popular notion that they're a hidebound, traditional, quiet lot. He stuck throughout his career to a belief that however dirty, smelly and stupid they were, the workers were 'decent'. And although they couldn't be *us*, they were certainly opposed to *them*, who, as his friend Isaac Deutscher put it, were 'hatching dark conspiracies against the decencies of Billy Brown of London Town'.[27] His conception of what made someone working-class was somewhat shaky – as Raymond Williams pointed out, he stayed throughout the writing of *The Road to Wigan Pier* with northern members of the Independent Labour Party and the Communist Party, but didn't see fit to mention them in the book, as, being politically conscious, they obviously weren't real workers.[28] Orwell's strictures against a cosmopolitan left have had a great influence upon those who appeal to an inherently decent and patriotic English working class against both the denationalising aims of Marxism and the effects of neoliberalism.

However, when looked at in detail, Orwell is not so much their ally as he first appears. Certainly, his rage against the middle-class left is real, and it has now grown into a barely sane outpouring of bigotry and paranoia, almost swamping the elements of truth in it. Those hosts in Wigan that he doesn't tell us about aren't representative socialists. The labour movement is best encapsulated by two fat-arsed hikers who got on his bus in (appropriately!) Letchworth Garden City, leading one passenger to mutter under their breath '*socialists*'. This carries him into the famous rants against every 'fruit-juice drinker, nudist, sandal-wearer, sex-maniac, Quaker, "Nature Cure" quack, pacifist and feminist' in England, all those 'vegetarians with wilting beards, Bolshevik commissars (half gangster, half gramophone), earnest ladies in sandals, shock-headed Marxists chewing polysyllables, escaped Quakers, birth-control fanatics, and Labour Party backstairs-crawlers',[29] all of them giving socialism a bad name. Aside from the influence on Richard Littlejohn and Jeremy Clarkson more than on Jon Cruddas or Billy Bragg, what is going on here? This is chiefly an invective against the off-putting bohemians, radicals and cultists that he considered turned politics into a matter of lifestyle choice. It's also an attack on the Soviet sympathies and mechanised aesthetics of the interwar modernists. He could have been thinking of Frank Pick when he claimed that 'the underlying notion of many socialists, I believe, is simply a hypertrophied sense of order. The present state of things offends them not because it causes misery, still less because it makes freedom impossible, but because it is untidy';[30] he could have been thinking of all the London aesthetes and émigrés that produced London Transport's posters and buildings or the GPO Film Unit's documentaries when he ranted about all the aficionados of the Soviet Union singing the praises of the Dnieper dam, the blast furnaces of Magnitogorsk or 'the latest canning factory in Moscow'. But look more closely at *The Road to Wigan Pier* or *The Lion and the Unicorn*, and you realise that the people who are considered to be revolted by all these lifestyle socialists and Sovietophiles are not your traditionalist, Sunday-roast proles, wedded to the *Racing Post* around the fire, saucy seaside postcards and a lifetime of selfless drudgery, who Orwell suspects are – especially in the North – usually going to be members of the trade unions voting Labour regardless. Instead they are a 'new class', made up of clerks, operatives in light industry and young women made to 'look like actresses' by Woolworths cosmetics; the people who live in semis and council estates on the outskirts of London and Birmingham; the people who inhabit the new landscape described in Priestley's *English Journey*, and that Frank Pick aimed to rationalise into a coherent order in his expansion programmes for the London Underground.

These 'classless' cohorts are not sympathetic to talk of class war, and nor, given that they already live a super-modern lifestyle of car, cinema and suburb, are they interested in the Soviets' celebration of old-hat symbols like tractors or dams. In fact, here Eric Arthur Blair is closer to Tony Blair, and his appeal to the 'aspirational' classes of post-industrial England, than he is to the traditionalist certainties of Blue Labour. In *The Lion and the Unicorn*, this is extended even further, to 'airmen and naval officers', whose patriotism 'an intelligent Socialist movement will use, instead of insulting it, as hitherto'.[31] The patriotism of the working classes, meanwhile, is grudging and reluctant;

in the same pamphlet, Orwell notes that pubs still refuse to serve pints to servicemen, and that workers retain a hatred for the very notion of a standing army. In fact, the polemical use of Orwell to bash the cosmopolitan left, with its fetish for jargon the ordinary man doesn't understand, and its preference for picturesque Commonwealth migrants rather than the indigenous salt of the earth, is surprisingly far from Orwell's intention. Orwell doesn't suggest that the left has a problem with alienating the working class, who he assumes will instinctively vote Labour anyway, but that they needlessly alienate a new and indeterminate suburban class, who share the bourgeoisie's pretensions but few of its privileges. What is happening in the current construction of the 'white working class', pining for 1940 and suspicious of immigrants, is a reversal of Orwell's analysis *of* 1940.

Orwell may have thought the working classes of the 1930s and 1940s were 'small-c conservative', but it's possible they were a good deal more internationalist in their political outlook than he let on. Reading Orwell's account, especially reading it carelessly, would lead you to the commonplace notion that radical socialism – Marxism in its various permutations, and in this case, the Communist Party of Great Britain – was entirely the preserve of North London intellectuals, the sort of people that read the *New Statesman*, experimented with crazy innovations like birth control or vegetarianism, knew about avant-garde painting and went hiking in Letchworth Garden City. Given that the Communist Party won their two MPs in 1945 in the East End of London and the Fife coalfield, and narrowly missed getting a third in the Rhondda Valley, rather than sweeping the board in Hampstead, this was clearly already a faulty assessment in Orwell's own time. The notion of the working class as inherently insular and anti-communist is comprehensively debunked in Victor Silverman's study, *Imagining Internationalism in American and British Labor, 1939–49*, which finds abundant evidence (in opinion polls, surveys, Mass Observation data, workers' accounts and popular histories) to show that the British working class in particular were deeply committed to a remaking of the world, along the lines of a socialist world federation rather more radical than Orwell's 'European Unity'.

During the war, Silverman writes,

> a collapsing of national and class concerns affected the way working people perceived themselves in the world. The commonly expressed idea of a 'New World' implied not only international reorganisation but also a reordering of domestic class relations, workplace relations, and internal union operations. Industrial unionism, one railway worker argued in 1942, provided the best model for world politics. Take a look at Europe to-day and you will see the dire results of the pre-war craft mentality in the foreign policy of nations. Poland refusing the aid of the Red Army, Belgium regarding the extension of the Maginot Line to the coast as an unfriendly act are but two crying examples.[32]

This is surprising stuff, given Orwell's harping on the workers' indifference to world affairs ('Parlay-voo?' asked one northern pub-goer when Orwell attempted to interest him in Hitler's remilitarisation of the Rhineland).

Silverman's examples show the degree to which, as Burgess's Welsh friend put it, people had gone 'bloody purple' during the war. 'Many people agreed with the intentions but probably doubted the realism of a group of Llanelly trade unionists during 1944 who called, "in the interests of civilisation and humanity", for the "abolition of national boundaries"'.[33] Not only were they internationalists, the workers were deeply sympathetic to the Soviet Union itself – even Orwell, in the *Lion and the Unicorn*, cites the 'Hands off Russia' campaign of 1920, when soldiers refused to fight with, and dockers refused to load munitions intended for, the White Armies in the anti-Bolshevik Civil War, as an exception to his rule that workers only cared for their own back gardens. Silverman's use of contemporary surveys and accounts makes clear that pro-Soviet sentiment was widespread in the 1930s and 40s, among the working class far more than among the bourgeoisie, or for that matter the intelligentsia. 'Even at government and TUC-sponsored events, class resentment articulated in pro-Soviet terms could not be contained. Perhaps most expressive were the number of voices raised in singing the Internationale as opposed to God Save the King ... Recognising the subversive power of the Internationale, the BBC did not play the song until forced to do so by public outcry.'[34] Lancastrian workers, the dumb and dignified beasts of burden that line the *Road to Wigan Pier*, thronged tours by Soviet leaders, workers, soldiers and trade unionists in the UK after the Soviets entered the war in 1941. One delegation leader, Nikolai Shvernik, was mobbed by Mancunian women; after his speech at a munitions plant a woman climbed on the stage, 'clung to his neck, kissed his forehead and then shouted "Come on girls, let's all kiss him."' Moments later, 'scores of elderly gray-haired women jumped onto the platform and struggled to kiss' Shvernik. Management convinced the women to go back to their seats, and 'in what may have been an attempt to cool their ardor, they all sang the Internationale'.[35]

That isn't to imply that workers weren't in many cases insular or xenophobic when it came to their own backyard. Silverman's main example here is the treatment by workers of Polish émigrés, many of them stateless after the war and trying to get jobs in factories and mines, but instead meeting abuse and even, in some unions, official censure, something that was encouraged by the Communist Party. A straightforward 'they're taking our jobs' racism, in a time of acute labour shortage, was justified by pro-Soviet (and additionally in Scotland, anti-Catholic) sentiments. 'Internationalism, the Poles learned, did not mean tolerance, and it apparently applied only to people far away. "For in no country", one Pole sadly explained, "is the word foreign so offensively pronounced."'[36] Although after 1948 the pro-Soviet ardour of British workers cooled somewhat, the Cold War was never popular, with the United States scoring below the Soviet Union in opinion polls for at least a decade after 1945. The NATO-founding foreign secretary and former dock leader Ernest Bevin 'blamed the left, and in a reflection of his English nationalism, "chiefly the Welsh" for opposition to Labour's demands for national sacrifice in order to assure its new relationship with the United States'.[37] The Labour government that put on the

Festival of Britain, introduced the welfare state and created the National Health Service was also a co-belligerent of the Cold War, and it's to this undercurrent in the Spirit of '45 that we will now turn.

Austerity London Celebrates Itself

If the 'English Revolution' as Orwell imagined it did not actually take place in 1945, what did? Aside from Ken Loach's film, '1945' (or rather the two Labour governments of 1945–50 and 1950–51) has entered the austerity-nostalgic imagination in two ways: one, as the regime that created the NHS, and two, as the regime that created the Festival of Britain. We will come to these two in turn, via the projects with which they are most associated – the post-war nationalisations and the 1951 Festival of Britain, both masterminded by former London County Council leader Herbert Morrison, and the NHS and the first wave of post-war housing, courtesy of the cabinet's resident committed socialist, Aneurin Bevan. Both of these figures were committed to their own version of Ingsoc, and both, in ways now usually ignored, harboured contrasting ideas about what to do with the legacy of Empire.

The Festival of Britain was not the product of the left-most parts of the Attlee government, far from it. The cabinet minister who took up the vague idea of a centenary equivalent to the original Great Exhibition at the Crystal Palace in 1951 was Herbert Morrison, who had been home secretary, deputy prime minister and eventually foreign secretary in the coalition and Labour governments of the

1940s and early 50s; however, he is possibly best remembered today for the near-decade in which he controlled the
London County Council. After winning the election in
1933, Morrison, a working-class Londoner, built a base so
strong that Labour were practically unchallenged until the
greatly expanded, less powerful Greater London Council
replaced the LCC in 1967. In a persistent, apocryphal anecdote, Morrison planned early on to achieve this by 'building
the Tories out of London', in other words through a mass
council housing programme that would keep Labour voters
in the inner city and secure their allegiance, while, perhaps
as an added bonus, encouraging dispossessed (and always
Tory-voting) landlords to leave the capital for somewhere
more easily exploited.

This makes Morrison, the grandfather of Peter Mandelson,
sound deeply radical: In the Attlee government, however,
he was a 'moderate', constantly urging caution after the
initial wave of reforms, so as not to alienate the southern
voters he knew so well. The nationalised industries that
Morrison created – in public transport, energy, coal, and
briefly, steel – were modelled wholesale on the London
Passenger Transport Board that he had created in the
early 1930s. That is, they were a form of public business.
Extravagant compensation was paid to buy off shareholders
and owners, but usually the same directors were, like Pick
and Ashfield, left in charge. These were – as miners would
find to their cost in the 1980s – answerable to the government rather than to their workers, with even apparently
left-wing cabinet members like Stafford Cripps abandoning
any semblance of the principle of workers' control. All the

'Morrisonian' nationalised industries were sold off in the 1980s and 90s, a popular measure initially, until they were run into the ground by the lucratively subsidised vultures we now know so well – Virgin Trains, Thames Water, et al. The awfulness of these successors imparts to the nationalised companies a radicalism they did not have at the time.

Similarly, there's not much in Morrison's career at the LCC that would point to him as the sponsor of the sudden outburst of openness, modernity and colour that the Festival represented. Although he had the crucial role in setting up the LPTB, the bureaucratic Maecenas of interwar London, LCC design under Morrison's watch was less radical even than Pick and Holden's taming and Anglicising of the modern movement. He greatly expanded the tenement-building programme of the conservative councils that had preceded him – strong, well-built, neo-Georgian flats, recognisable all over inner London from Plumstead to White City, with beautifully cut, uniform signage, the LCC crest,

Building the Tories out of London: the LCC tenement

and a slightly expressionist dash to the balconies and walk-ways as notable as the Georgian proportions of the windows. This, and comparable schemes in Liverpool and Leeds, was the real mass housing of the interwar years, conservative and centralised around often rather indistinct 'greens', all of them now car parks, but often equipped with amenities like pubs, shops, cafes and launderettes. The most radical examples, like the huge, whitewashed Ossulston Estate in Somers Town, were monumental, heroic structures on the model of the grand courts of 'Red Vienna'. Other public buildings of the LCC, like St Martin's College in Charing Cross Road, or the Central Fire Station in Lambeth, evince a bricky, modernised classicism of the sort that is very fashionable among twenty-first-century architects. But this is no preparation for what Morrison, with the LCC's help, would do in 1951.

The Festival is now so mythologised that it is hard to see it without the rose-tinted spectacles of austerity nostalgia. It consisted, first, of a dozen or so temporary buildings on various themes, usually devoted to giving a modern and progressive face to the battered, indebted country being celebrated. Sea and Ships, designed by Basil Spence, celebrated naval power; the Lion and the Unicorn, as we've seen, with its great frieze by Edward Bawden, celebrated British specificity and eccentricity; the Telekinema, by the hard-line 1930s modernist Wells Coates, was a precursor to the National Film Theatre built nearby a few years later; and Power and Production, designed by the Lancastrian George Grenfell Baines, celebrated the still extant industrial might. These pavilions were spread out informally amid bunting, brightly coloured decorations and organic, Scandinavian-influenced light fittings on Hugh Casson's informal, anti-hierarchical layout, on overhead walkways and pedestrian paths around the three most famous buildings – Ralph Tubbs's Dome of Discovery, the Skylon and the only permanent one, the Royal Festival Hall. The latter came courtesy of the LCC's architects' department after a modernist internal coup. It was principally designed by Robert Matthew and the émigré Peter Moro, under the decisive influence of Berthold Lubetkin's decorative, humorous version of high-minded socialist modernism.

After the Tories returned to power, despite winning less votes than Labour, in a 1951 election that the government were pressed to call by George VI, Churchill acted on his stated intention to demolish this exercise in 'three-dimensional socialist propaganda'. In 1961, after years standing derelict as a surface car park, the Festival site had imposed upon it the grossly monolithic, stripped classical Shell Centre, its both wan and pompous offices spreading out to the riverfront, and the faintly pitiful tower – like a taller, more conservative and less stylish version of Senate House – dominating the London skyline until other skyscrapers grew to complement it.

Accordingly, the Festival of Britain is mooned over as an absence, a future that didn't come to pass; indeed, specialists of the future that didn't come to pass inevitably make reference to it, with even Julian House of Ghost Box talking of his aim to reproduce the never-recorded sound of the sort of avant-garde music that Festival-goers would have heard in 1951. That shouldn't obscure the fact that the young architects and artists who would later go on to found brutalism and pop art loathed the Festival, as an ingratiating, technically backward piece of whimsy. Look, James Stirling demanded, at the difference between the Crystal Palace of 1851 – a building so radical it took decades to be fully understood, and more than a century to be fully assimilated into the architectural repertoire – and the Festival of 1951, a tame, pleasant affair that essentially replicated the jocular modernism of the 1930 Stockholm Exhibition.

The unfairness of this judgement – who could really have a problem with something so obviously humane as the Festival Hall? – may be explained by the way that more disturbing, aggressive, mediated or avant-garde forms of modern art and architecture were kept out of the Festival. According to architectural historian Christoph Grafe, works by Richard Hamilton, a key figure for the pop artists and the brutalists, were specifically vetoed by the curator of the Festival's art exhibition, Herbert Read. The Festival was to be the preserve of 'romantic moderns', not aggressive modernists. This was modernism as consensus, not dissonance.

What Grafe's account makes clear, though, is how successful the LCC's architectural 'left' were in wresting the project from the austere bureaucratic architects of the 1930s. In the original post-war plan for London, this former industrial site in Lambeth was to be transformed into a cultural centre, not via informally placed modernist pavilions and free-flowing space, but through strongly centralised, high-rise, stripped classical buildings on the model of Senate House, and again designed by Charles Holden. In that sense, the Shell Centre's ideas, at least, precede the

Festival buildings whose floor area it squats upon. The Festival's radicalism, and much of its popularity, is more explicable when one realises that it directly replaced, here, this sort of pomposity – a stodgy classicism which would get its revenge on the Festival's site after 1951, when the Shell Centre was built.

What you can see there now is dominated by developments which post-date the Festival. East of the original site, the Festival Hall was complemented in the mid-1960s with the 'South Bank Centre' (the Queen Elizabeth Hall, the Purcell Room and the Hayward Gallery), in the 1970s with the National Theatre, and in the 2000s with a series of retail buildings in front of and alongside the Festival Hall. Most important of all, it became a truly public building when all of its foyers were opened to the public all day and all evening under 'Red' Ken Livingstone, head of the Greater London Council in the early 1980s. A great deal of the public affection for the building – the 'People's Palace' – really comes from this act of opening-up, where the generous foyers, previously restricted to those who had paid for a ticket, were made available at all times of day for more or less anyone to do what they liked there. In short, the Festival Hall as a really socialist space comes from a combination of 1940s post-war consensus architecture and 1980s 'loony left' local politics.

This is perhaps somewhat withered today, as a series of gastronomic 'street markets', relational aesthetics add-ons, expensive concert halls, wi-fi foyers and shops selling austerity nostalgia knick-knacks take over the space, while the RFH staff move in on political meetings; but it is still

The South Bank eats itself

a strikingly free and public space by London's standards. Livingstone's GLC made the Festival Hall much more radical than it was supposed to be. Originally the Festival, according to Grafe, was the legacy both of the 'internal colonisation' of Toynbee Hall, the late-Victorian East End social centre where concerned middle-class Londoners would descend to assist 'darkest England', and of the Houses of the People, Co-operative Halls and Workers Clubs set up by the organised working class itself, and reflected that tension.

The Festival's main organiser, the *News Chronicle* editor Gerald Barry, headed a committee manned by some deeply establishment figures, some of whom we have come across – Kenneth Clark, Stephen Tallents – and others we have not, such as John Gielgud and 'Red Tory' (in today's language) and educational reformer Rab Butler. Barry claimed that 'we envisage this as the people's show, not organised arbitrarily for them to enjoy, but put on largely by them, by us all, as an expression of a way of life in which we believe'. In reality, as Michael Frayn pointed out, 'the people were hardly involved ... nothing about the result [suggests] that the working classes were anything more than the lovably human but essentially inert objects of benevolent administration.'[38] The result was torn between the unashamed project of being 'a new meeting place of intelligent citizens' and 'an experience of being together and being equal ... the representation of a new, egalitarian society'.[39] Pre-Livingstone, the Hall was the least egalitarian part of the entire Festival. Much was made of one of the building workers attending one of the first concerts after the Hall opened, but with compulsory evening dress and no public access to the foyers, it can't have seemed terribly egalitarian until the 1980s. The architectural critic Robert Maxwell, sympathetic to the brutalists, described the Festival Hall as early as the 1960s as being the product of a time when 'the English played at being social democrats', implying that even under Harold Wilson Britain had returned to its mercantile roots. As Grafe explains, the brutalist additions to the site, with their oblique angles, spaced-out seating and avant-garde or pop programme (Syd Barrett's Pink Floyd were one of the first acts to play the Queen Elizabeth Hall) were in some ways shifts away from the big, inclusive, humanitarian *Gemeinschaft* of the Festival towards a more fragmented, private world, an aestheticisation of the traumatic impact of the twentieth century on the psyche rather than an attempt to transcend it – the English sensibility as described by J. G. Ballard, not George Orwell. As early as the 1960s, this place looked dated.

So why did observers see in it something so utopian and egalitarian? The German architect Karl Wimmenauer, after clapping his eyes upon the Royal Festival Hall in 1951, enthused that 'England is perhaps about to become the most social country in the world', pioneering a 'humanist social- ism' well in advance of anything that was being planned by, say, West Germany.[40] Much of this can simply be put down to the building itself and its successful Anglicisation, without compromise this time, of pure modernist ideas. The building, especially after it was completed in the 1960s (for over a decade, a temporary, decorative south facade had hidden unfinished spaces), is as remarkable, sweep- ing and free a modernist space as you can find anywhere. Around the 'egg' of the main hall, a 'box' is filled with great glazed rooms, with no programmatic use, through which – especially post-Livingstone – the visitor can just wander around enjoying the changes of level, the fine materials, the sense of sudden light, air and openness, or simply the fact that for once they're not being importuned to buy anything. The front facade transparently shows what the building is, a series of unusually large and generous foyers around a central hall, which protrudes at the top to give the building its arc-like silhouette. But if this is very like what one could expect from a late 1920s Palace of Culture in Moscow, the details are wholly the designers' own, and deeply English. The famous carpet is pretty, decorative, and in the sort of unobtrusive green that a Pevsner would call quintessentially English; the handrails, beautifully carved, are grooved so that you are encouraged to run your fingers along their surface as you walk up and down the stairs; there is bronze, frosted glass, neo-Victorian *lettres ornées* typography, and in the hall itself, flamboyant, whimsical neo-Regency balconies. The whole gives off a feeling of warmth, domesticity even.

Unlike the designers of London Transport such as Charles Holden, the LCC's architects did not temper their modernism, with no hint of classical roots behind the sweeping space – so the designers' Englishry is even more pronounced, seeming like a series of wilful touches intended to delight and amuse, once again with that implicit assurance that there is something inherently marvellous and moderate about England. The later brutalists who were so disappointed by the Festival must have been itching for revenge, long before they linked the South Bank Centre's brackish forms to the Festival Hall – though even then, there was great care taken not to overwhelm the earlier building, but merely to supplement and complement its massing, while rejecting everything about its aesthetics.

The forgotten result of the Festival of Britain's architecture, though, is that part of it much more permanent than the South Bank, as permanent as the Festival Hall: the Lansbury Estate. It was named after George Lansbury, the former Labour leader and one-time head of the local council, Poplar. Lansbury was a much more left-wing figure than Morrison, even going to prison for refusing to implement cuts in his borough's social programmes. The Lansbury Estate was Anglicised modernism taken beyond the Festival's joyfully whimsical details into outright Cockney retro, evidently considered appropriate in this (then) dockside area. Most of the housing consisted of pitched-roofed stock-brick terraces in squares, open on the south side, lining slightly formal little village greens, most of them now given at least some token fencing-off. Aside from the clipped modernist details around the doors and the lack of any period ornament, this was quite obviously just a 'normal' bit of London, differing from the template mainly in its avoidance of the pokiness of the average East End terrace. There are two churches, one Anglican, stern and Scandomodernist, the other Catholic, a monumental, stepped, obsessively detailed brick monster by one of the Gilbert Scott dynasty.

All of this is grouped around Chrisp Street Market, where architect Frederick Gibberd, hardly known for his whimsy, gives full rein to a melange of nostalgic details mashed with modernist planning so quaint as to warm Alexandra Harris's heart. The buildings of this precinct, organised around a still-bustling market, may be *en pilotis* and may be pedestrianised, but otherwise they're bursting with decorative brickwork, neo-Regency bay windows, pitched roofs and other little touches; the Festival Pub is a central part of the whole thing, suggesting that the architecture of East End social reform had moved on a great deal since Toynbee Hall. Marking the entrance to the estate was a clock tower, originally intended to give a view of the docks but closed to the public within a couple of years. It all became a normal part of the East End, and although the inhabitants have often changed over the generations, its design still conveys the sense of slightly uneasy, knees-up nostalgia that so often emerges where intellectual meets Cockney. None of this has ever been listed, and at the

The 'Festival District': the Lansbury Estate

time of writing, it is in danger of partial demolition and replacement.

The contrast between the two parts of the Festival is instructive. The Festival itself was experienced as egalitarian in the way its buildings were organised, through Hugh Casson's Swedish-style free plan, a novel experience for Britain in 1951: an urban space that was not a rigid system of streets and houses, with a strict divide between public and private, but a seamless thing where you could weave in and out, below and above the buildings (ironically, the least public aspect of it, open in 1951 only to paying customers, was the sole surviving building, the Festival Hall). It's this, as well as the cheery, semi-retro motifs applied to the modernist architecture and the slightly raised-eyebrow techno-optimism of the exhibits themselves, that ingratiated visitors with a previously suspect modernist project. However, the exact same ideas, when assembled a few miles north and east, in Poplar, came to mean something

else. The Lansbury Estate follows very similar principles –
the freedom of movement through space, an egalitarianism where the district was designed so as not to have dark
corners or any part wealthier or poorer than another, and
a similar yoking of modernism and 'romantic modernist'
details. Both, also, later got as neighbours more confident,
more ruthlessly modern structures – the Festival Hall being
joined onto the Queen Elizabeth Hall and the Hayward
Gallery, the Lansbury Estate being a footpath away from
Ernő Goldfinger's rigorous, brutalist Brownfield Estate.

The South Bank has had its problems, but it has never
faced a funding squeeze comparable to that which Tower
Hamlets Council, the Lansbury Estate's owners, has suf-
fered for decades. Little bits of the Festival Hall have
not been sold off at a massive discount to its users. What
makes this especially sad is that the Festival Hall was just
a showcase of the possibilities of social democratic Britain,
a fragment of an exhibit, a test case for what everything
was meant to be like. On the other hand, Lansbury was the
version of it that people actually lived in, and have done
now for generations. Rather than being packaged, like the
Festival Hall, as a repository of kitsch and trinkets (it is to
the 2010s what the Albert Hall was to the 1960s, an image
of a somehow better era that you still wouldn't necessarily
want to live in), the Lansbury Estate is almost forgotten.

The Empire Disappears

Beyond building a lot of very decent tenements and commissioning a Festival on the South Bank of the Thames,

the career of Herbert Morrison encompassed a tenure as foreign secretary; after being appointed, he immediately asked for a biography of the great nineteenth-century imperialist statesman, Lord Palmerston. While the Empire seemed to have disappeared from British iconography as seen in the Festival, it certainly didn't disappear from the Attlee government's actual political horizon. Although India had been freed and bloodily partitioned, as had the more recently acquired British colony of Palestine, the rest of the intercontinental British Empire remained intact. Not only the de facto independent 'dominions' of the 'Commonwealth' such as Canada, Australia, South Africa and New Zealand and now India, Pakistan and Burma, but great swathes of Africa and Asia – the latter just wrested back from the Japanese, and the site of huge, popular and often Communist-led resistance movements as soon as the war was over. In 1951, when Labour left office, Britain had full control over what is now Cyprus, Malta, Jamaica, Trinidad, St Lucia, Iraq, Singapore, Hong Kong, Malaysia, Somalia, Kenya, Ghana, Nigeria, Zimbabwe, Tanzania, Malawi, Sri Lanka, among others. And yet these hardly featured as part of 'Britain' or its 'identity' in its Festival of itself, in notable contrast with earlier Expos in London, such as the Wembley Exhibition of 1925, otherwise the Festival's obvious precursor. This is especially strange given that the Labour leadership, particularly Morrison and Bevin, were convinced social imperialists.

Labour in fact represented the culmination, not the rejection, of the ideas of social imperialism. 'With a nationalist, Ernest Bevin, as Foreign Secretary, internationalism was

relegated to the backbenches during the Labour governments of 1945–51', while Cold War pressures enabled the
party to bring the imperialists' 'dream of national service to
fruition'.[41] Although the National Service Act was supposedly passed in order to maintain the British occupying force
in the British-mandated parts of Germany and Austria, the
newly conscripted youth of the austerity years were soon
being sent abroad, to fight ruthless wars against Communists
in Malaya and then, soon after Labour were overthrown,
against the Mau Mau in Kenya, where extensive use was
made of collective punishment and concentration camps
(Britain had, after all, invented these during the Boer War).
The excuse for some interventions was the imperatives of
the Cold War, given that resistance movements particularly in Asia were often Communist, as Orwell could have
warned us. Although Attlee may have averted World War
III by refusing to let the Americans nuke China in revenge
for the People's Liberation Army humbling them in the
Korean War, he is more responsible for the formation of the
Atlantic alliance than any other European politician. Labour
Atlanticists like to credit the creation of NATO more precisely to Ernest Bevin, who devised it to 'keep the Germans
down, the Americans in and the Russians out', safeguard-
ing democracy, freedom and suchlike in the process. When
he wasn't sponsoring and speaking for modernist Festivals
of British identity, Herbert Morrison was Bevin's linear
successor, with, as one American report sneeringly had it at
the time, 'the Cockney's traditional hatred of foreigners'.
Much as he intended nationalisation to stop with steel, he
hoped for decolonisation to end with India.

In the process, he would use a metaphor not unlike Orwell's notion of the colonies as the cats and dogs kept by the British family. 'Giving [the African colonies] premature independence' would be 'like giving a child of ten a latchkey, a bank account and a shotgun'. Robert Skidelsky, writing from a position sympathetic to this idea, notes its total failure in reality:

Until they grew up, [the colonies] might help Britain's balance of payments. At the Colonial Office from 1945 to 1950 the Fabian Arthur Creech Jones took up Joseph Chamberlain's idea of 'colonial development'. A conscious attempt was made to develop the African colonies as a source of foodstuffs and raw materials and export outlets for British industry. Labour set up a Colonial Development Corporation to channel money to the African colonies. One of its famously disastrous efforts was the groundnuts scheme in Tanganyika, which was expected to provide margarine to the British consumer. It cost 36 million without producing a single commercial nut. The empire marketing boards [not to be confused with the abolished EMB] were used to purchase sugar from the West Indies on long-term contracts at below-market prices. Colonial development included training Africans for 'self-government'. Nigeria and the Gold Coast (later Ghana) received constitutions in 1946 which set up legislatures with limited African participation and less power. This model was followed throughout Britain's African colonies.[42]

The economic disaster of social imperialism, when it was finally properly tried, was surely noticed by the City of London and other historic backers of British mercantile capitalism. The farcical groundnuts scheme was spurred by Bevin's attempt to maintain the British Empire, believing that with the loss of India, sub-Saharan Africa could act as the powerhouse of British economic recovery, exploited in order to prevent Britain from becoming wholly subservient to the United States. This attempt did not end as a matter of principle, it ended because it was utterly inept. To funnel money from the metropolis to the periphery was no longer considered something worth risking, particularly as Britain was crushed under its colossal American debt, at least until the Marshall Plan saved it. Soon, it would prove possible for European and American capital to benefit greatly from the extraction and exploitation of African resources without the need for nominal control or pledges of allegiance to the Queen. Perhaps in that context, some in the Labour government – such as Aneurin Bevan – had other ideas about how to reconcile socialism with Britain staying a 'Great Power'.

Nothing Is Too Good

Most of the time, when people on the left talk about the Spirit of '45, what they really mean is the Spirit of Nye Bevan. When the Health and Social Care bill was passed into law at the start of 2012, it triggered one of those ultimately impotent 'hashtag campaigns' unleashed so frequently on Twitter, where – the notion is – by clicking on the tag used by thousands of people, the strength of collective opinion becomes manifest. There was previously a very popular hashtag, #welovetheNHS, launched in response to the claim by opponents of Obama's 'public option' in US healthcare that the British National Health Service was a widely hated basket case. Here each contributor preceded or succeeded the # with an anecdote, crammed into 140 characters, about something the NHS had done for themselves or their relatives free of charge. The tag when the Health and Social Care Act was passed was less heart-warming – an apparently cryptic #lowerthanvermin, usually accompanied by an expression of hatred of the Conservative Party and predictions of the dire consequences of a soon-to-be privately operated NHS. It was similarly popular, however: you could scroll down page after page after page of invective if you clicked on the tag.

The source of #lowerthanvermin is a speech made by the minister of health, Aneurin Bevan, at a Labour Party rally on 4 July 1948, on the eve of the launch of the free, wholly nationalised National Health Service that he had devised and presented to the public. Although Bevan had the backing of the prime minister and some anticipatory backup from the cross-party acceptance of the Beveridge Report, which committed the government to some form of universal health care, the shape the NHS took was inspired, according to Bevan's account, by the self-organised, free-at-the-point-of-use health service set up by organised workers in Tredegar – the small mining town in the Sirhowy Valley where he was born and raised, and where he began his political career. Forced through despite the opposition of the British Medical Association, whose members resented the prospect of becoming state employees rather than independent small businessmen, the NHS unified and nationalised the various municipal, religious and charitable hospitals, something which was at least as important to Bevan – in its elimination of profit-seeking in health – as the free cost of care to patients. It is possibly the most radical institution ever built in the UK. But the speech at which Bevan announced its inception is remembered not so much for his trumpeting of this achievement, as for the painful reminders of what made it necessary.

> No attempts at ethical or social seduction can eradicate from my heart a deep burning hatred of the Tory Party that inflicted those bitter experiences on me. So far as I am concerned they are lower than vermin. They condemned millions of first-class people to semi-starvation ... The Tories are pouring out money in propaganda of all sorts and are hoping in this sustained mass suggestion to eradicate all memory of what we went through. But I warn you, they have not changed – if they have, they are slightly worse than they were.[43]

What he had in mind were people like his father, David Bevan, who, his biographer Niklaus Thomas-Symonds points out,[44] was choked to death by pneumoconiosis (a lung condition caused by long-term inhalation of coal dust) but no compensation was paid to him, because it was not classified as an industrial disease under the Workmen's Compensation Act. Bevan himself, who left school at fourteen, was dismissed from his job as a miner as a 'troublemaker', and witnessed throughout his early life ill-health, grinding, unsafe work, and appalling living conditions, while being fully aware that others were doing very well off the proceeds.

It's hard to imagine any other speech, from this or any other moment, being resurrected at the moment that the Conservatives moved to privatise the NHS. The phrase even features on T-shirts. The speech, and Bevan himself, are now a part of folk memory. This MP for a small mining constituency in South Wales had defied party discipline so frequently that he was actually expelled in 1939, for advocating a French-style 'Popular Front' between the Labour Party and the Communists; notwithstanding, Attlee appointed him as minister of health (also with responsibility for housing) in 1945. After resigning in 1951 over the issue of prescription charges, he would this time lead the Labour left, now dubbed 'Bevanites', before breaking with them in turn in 1957 over the issue of nuclear disarmament, something usually put down to the compromises incumbent on his role as shadow foreign secretary. He died relatively young, in 1960, leaving the British left with one of its few great myths.

As a socialist politician Bevan was intent as much as possible on doing things, and this meant doing them in the Labour Party, which was his political vehicle from the outset as a Monmouthshire councillor. Compared with those other leaders of the Labour left – the pure but ineffectual James Maxton, the permanently frustrated Tony Benn – Bevan is responsible for one titanic, albeit now eviscerated, achievement.

Bevan drew on a mass of ideas, from the Beveridge Report, through miners' self-organised health care to the

modernist Health Centres set up by more radical councils in the late 1930s, such as the famous Finsbury Health
Centre that appeared on a wartime poster as a promise of
post-war Britain. He also discarded alternative models,
such as the 'preventative' care advocated by the Peckham
Health Centre. All in all, a Labour movement habitually
regarded as hidebound and conservative managed to build
an institution in many ways more radical than anything
then envisaged in France, Germany or Scandinavia. The
NHS was a great political idea. Bevan had to forego parts
of his programme in order to achieve his goal of a system
entirely publicly owned and free at the point of use –
specifically, by allowing doctors still to charge non-NHS
patients and to work semi-independently, allowing the
existence of a parallel, private health care system that
would, eventually, have consequences for the NHS itself.
However, it would take more than half a century for the
NHS's main principles to be seriously eroded. What Bevan
called the 'language of priorities' and the order of compromises appears to have been fully worth it in this case.

Many accounts – most recently, Lynsey Hanley's
memoir/history *Estates* – have good words to say for
'Bevan Houses', strongly built suburban terraces and semis,
with two bathrooms and lots of space. Hanley also points
out that Bevan envisaged the country's housing needs
being met by a publicly-owned National Housing Service,
as universal and comprehensive as the NHS for health.
Bevan's major speech on housing declared that 'we will be
judged by the quality of these homes',[45] not their quantity.
The speech was given in 1946 at the opening of Spa Green,

an attractive, ultra-modern housing estate in Finsbury designed by Berthold Lubetkin, and was a retort to those demanding greater speed, greater prefabrication, and if necessary smaller homes and fewer bathrooms to make greater numbers possible. The National Housing Service was glimpsed in the mooted but never seriously explored National Building Corporation, which Bevan initially advocated but quickly retreated from, in view of probable local authority opposition and their undeniably superior knowledge of local terrain and conditions. Bevan's adversary here, the chancellor and later housing minister Hugh Dalton, promptly cut Bevan's specification for at least two toilets per household. Bevan's partner, Jennie Lee, later wondered:

> Why did Hugh Dalton deride Nye's insistence? ... Did he not know how much it mattered if there was sickness in the family, or maybe an elderly parent to be cared for as well as the children? Dalton by birth and upbringing belonged to a privileged world. He had not the sympathy or imagination enough to bridge that gap.[46]

Ironically, though, Labour's real embrace of cost-cutting and rapid construction came in the 1960s, under Richard Crossman, formerly a passionate 'Bevanite'.

If 'Bevan Houses', essentially council flats with specifications on the level of Mayfair mansion blocks, never quite came to pass, they do exist in fragments. It is deeply apt, and touching to the socialist nostalgic, that Bevan's speech insisting on quality above all else in housing was given at one of Lubetkin's estates. Lubetkin is to British social architecture

Aneurin Bevan's future London: Spa Green

what Bevan is to socialism, a great heroic myth. Like
Bevan, he embodied the radical fringe of a usually reformist movement, and they would both find some difficulty in
surviving amidst the much less idealistic direction that the
post-war settlement would take after 1951. Lubetkin's, or
rather the Tecton Group's, work was a direct application
of early Soviet ideas – the 'social condenser', where public
functions would be served through overlapping, intersect-
ing public spaces, and housing would be closely integrated
with facilities like libraries, health centres, schools, social
clubs and (in Lubetkin's version) pubs.

Typically for the decade, the 1930s versions of this were
mostly apartment blocks, such as the famous Highpoint I
and Highpoint II, and aimed at a middle-class clientele,
bar a popular side line in constructivist zoos (London,
Whipsnade and Dudley). This work showed a gradual move
away from strict, hard-line and luxuriously appointed modernism, very much on the model of the firm's continental

examples, into a whimsical and seemingly 'English' love for paradox and pattern. The second of the Highpoints abandoned all-white surfaces for a pattern of brick and tile, and provoked the purists by placing two cast Athenian caryatids at the building's entrance. The 1938 Finsbury Health Centre similarly takes a step back from the pure blare and aggression of Le Corbusier or the Moscow constructivists who Lubetkin had hitherto taken as his models. With its neo-Victorian typeface, symmetry and slight monumentality (especially for what is actually a tiny building), this is a dry run for the Festival Hall. Ironically, many of the South Bank's architects, such as Peter Moro and later, Denys Lasdun, had been among Lubetkin's comrades in Tecton. All of Lubetkin's works are pivotal for austerity nostalgia of every political and aesthetic stripe. Alexandra Harris uses the Highpoint II caryatids to enlist him as a 'Romantic Modern'; People Will Always Need Plates do mugs and tea towels of nearly all these buildings; and, closer to Lubetkin's own politics, images of the Finsbury Health Centre have been carried as banners on anti-austerity demonstrations. Finsbury was nearly sold off after the Health and Social Care bill passed, and survived as a local health centre thanks to a large, lively campaign supported by the local MP, Jeremy Corbyn.

After the war, however, with the Spa Green, Priory Green and Bevin Court estates, all three around Finsbury, and the Hallfield Estate in Paddington, Lubetkin would completely reject any hint of austerity in favour of a new modernist style of generosity and surface. The famous declaration that 'nothing is too good for ordinary people'

(sometimes attributed to Bevan himself) was made about
Finsbury Health Centre, but it could equally be applied
to the way that Lubetkin and what was left of Tecton –
soon reorganised into the more prosaic Skinner, Bailey
and Lubetkin – developed in explicit, utterly ignored
opposition to all the main trends of post-war British
architecture.

Lubetkin, who had moved to Gloucestershire in the early
1950s to run a pig farm, infuriated by the rejection of his
visionary plans for the Durham Coalfield new town of
Peterlee, concentrated his energies on trying to adapt (or,
as opponents claimed, mask) the extremely low budgets set
for his mass housing projects, by creating rhetorical images
of symmetry, alignment and unity. This was aimed against,
on the one hand, the picturesque fragmentation of 'people's detailing' projects like the Lansbury Estate – cutesy
and ingratiating, in his view – and on the other what he
saw as the egotism and aggression of brutalism, which is
curious, given that his 1930s work was canonical for young
London architects in the 1960s. Spa Green was the first
foreshadowing of this strange, late riposte. Three blocks
in a little park, they are dressed in brown and cream tiles,
picked out in bright colours, and with an interest in pattern
which Lubetkin, who had grown up in Georgia, claimed
was inspired by the Caucasian carpets he had seen in his
youth. The lowest of the three blocks curves around in
an irregular squiggle, designed to show off the advanced
engineering of collaborator Ove Arup. Each entrance is
marked by impressive ramps, louvres and signs, to give
the required sense of importance, to signal that this is

something other than box-ticking en masse, a mere empty-ing of the waiting list. Priory Green went on to replicate this in a denser, less attractive fashion, but at Bevin Court, Lubetkin would almost flail against the limits of the project. A Y-shaped block of flats without balconies, it is arranged in a white/grey/red pattern around a Picassoesque mural by the painter-architect Peter Yates, and the most astonish-ing, violent, melodramatic staircase, the most constructivist space designed anywhere outside of 1920s Moscow. Only an escape staircase, with most residents using the lifts, it is gratuitously magnificent, utterly unnecessary, designed solely to inspire pleasure and awe.

This would be the model for two huge projects in Bethnal Green, the Dorset Estate and the Cranbrook Estate. Neither is listed, as Lubetkin had by this time moved even further away from acceptable modernist architecture, but they are even more obsessive and remarkable: huge slabs and towers arranged around tree-lined monumental routes

Municipal Rococo – a staircase at the Cranbrook Estate

that seem to have escaped from eighteenth-century France, all of them with riotously individual, sensual and vertiginous staircases. Everywhere, though, you can see Skinner, Bailey and Lubetkin straining against the Crossman-imposed limits on overspending on mere council housing. Extreme, flamboyant spatial ideas are lined by wan council lawns, dazzling patterns are executed in cheap tile and brick, the staircases are clad in the nearest the architects could get to a shiny stone, now coated in layers of dust, leading to claustrophobic vandal-proof lifts – a state obviously aided and abetted by decades of neglect. All these features are statements of collectivity and abundance in an era of increasingly atomised consumerism, heroic attempts to wish the socialist community back into being. They're a bid by a committed and slightly Stalinist Communist to bring into being with the slightest of means the original promise of the socialist future. As such, they stand much more closely for the eventual fate of 1945's more expansive dreams than most of the housing that actually resulted. For someone like Lubetkin, the housing of the welfare state fell considerably short of what he'd hoped, and instead his architecture strains to achieve the impossible.[47]

However, while the obviously somewhat gimcrack nature of the designs meant that they did not, initially, form part of the Lubetkin canon or the modernist revival pantheon, Skinner, Bailey and Lubetkin's late estates are exceptionally well located. In fact, the Dorset Estate and Sivill House are just around the corner from the austerity-nostalgia store Labour and Wait, in Shoreditch. Google 'Sivill House' and you'll find that the tower of this municipal housing estate – so achingly Old Labour that its blocks are named after the Tolpuddle Martyrs – is a thoroughly des res, where a one-bedroom ex-council flat is likely to set you back a quarter of a million quid. The adverts for flats there, at RightMove and the like, will usually point out as one of the tower's Unique Selling Points the fact that it was designed by the great Berthold Lubetkin. The reddest of the red can still be sold off: all that's required is a cash-strapped council, or a tenant with enough in the bank to snap it up on Right to Buy. And the austerity nostalgia industry makes sure that the investment will be lucrative.

Towards a Non-Aligned Nuclear Britain

Bevin Court's original name would be an early casualty of the Cold War. Since in front of the block was an early Victorian square where Lenin had briefly lived in exile, Tecton provided a memorial for this in the form of a bust, enclosed by one of the strange, flowing, geometric sculptures that Lubetkin had been using to make entrances to new housing estates. Repeatedly vandalised by the British Union of Fascists with antisemitic graffiti, Lubetkin regularly replaced the bust (mass-produced in the USSR) until eventually Finsbury Council gave up and renamed 'Lenin Court' as Bevin Court, having only to change two letters. This supplanting of the Soviet internationalist with one of the Cold War's earliest warriors could not be more apt. Bevan, his near-namesake and cabinet colleague, had other ideas about what British socialist foreign policy might be. Without ever completely departing from the horizons of social imperialism, these ideas were so extensive, and so strange, that they are worth examining in detail.

The familiar story is that Cold War imperatives – rearmament, the Korean War, and of course the British Atomic Bomb – led to Hugh Gaitskell as chancellor imposing prescription charges on the new NHS, a move which Bevan couldn't countenance. He resigned and brought the government down with him, leading to thirteen years in the wilderness. The story as Nicklaus Thomas-Symonds tells it is rather different, with Gaitskell the uncompromising ideologue, and Bevan a pragmatist straining to accommodate himself until eventually pushed too far. By this account, Bevan was hardly an enemy of the Cold War at its inception, or of Britain's involvement in it. He supported rearmament, he supported Britain sending troops to Korea; he supported the founding of NATO, and he even, it transpires, supported the development of the British bomb. But when Gaitskell put together a budget with wildly inflated figures for defence – so high that Bevan claimed, with reason, that the government wouldn't even be physically able to spend the money in the time allocated – and then imposed charges for prescriptions, Bevan, who had committed himself to resigning in the event of any NHS charges, was practically forced to step down. This wasn't a melodramatic flounce, but a defeat by a far more ruthless and driven political operator.

Bevan's relationship to the Cold War is important, as he devoted himself largely to international affairs after 1951; he would have become foreign secretary if Labour had won the 1955 or 1959 elections, and would very probably have taken the same position if he'd lived to join Wilson's first cabinet. Similarly to Orwell, his contemporary at *Tribune*, Bevan was a 'revolutionary patriot' during the war. He was heavily critical of the wartime coalition for its restrictions on civil liberties, as well as for its military blunders, especially the lateness in starting a second front in Europe to aid the Red Army. Also, significantly, he asked questions in Parliament about the severe measures the coalition government imposed on its Indian colony, with almost arbitrary death sentences for potential acts of 'sabotage' like cutting telephone wires. 'Collective fines are imposed on areas for suspected sabotage. A military officer over a certain rank can take life in trying to protect property'[48] – this campaign of wartime repression culminated in the calamitous Bengal famine of 1943. Nonetheless, after the war, Bevan spoke of Britain's 'moral leadership of the world' while it starved millions in Bengal, ruthlessly suppressed an insurgency in Malaya and facilitated the chaotic, bloody partitions in India and Israel–Palestine. However, all this was in the service of a never realised grand project.

Bevan appears to have been committed to a version of the Non-Aligned Movement – that is, to something resembling the alternative bloc that was forming in the 1950s of non-NATO, non-Warsaw Pact countries like Yugoslavia, India, Indonesia and Ghana, which did not have, and explicitly refused, the 'nuclear umbrella' of either the United States or the Soviet Union – although Bevan's conception of non-alignment involved a central role both for nuclear weapons and for the maintenance of British military power. In this, Bevan was immediately at variance with the Labour left grouping later known as 'Bevanites', who generally favoured abandonment of any British role as a world power. In a meeting at which Bevan was not present, his near-namesake Ernest Bevin insisted that 'we've got to have the bloody Union Jack on top of' the nuclear bomb. Later, with the notorious 1957 conference speech where he asked whether anti-nuclear campaigners wanted to see Britain go 'naked to the conference table', Bevan explicitly disassociated himself from the unilateral disarmament advocated by his close allies such as Michael Foot, Ian Mikardo and Richard Crossman. This apparent flailing can be explained: his real position was always the same, nukes for non-alignment.

Bevin's bomb with a bloody Union Jack on top was reimagined to become Bevan's bomb for the protection of the post-colonial, democratic socialist Non-Aligned Bloc, including Yugoslavia, India, Ghana, et al. Yet it is hard to suppose that any of these countries would have preferred to be protected by a British 'deterrent' rather than a Soviet or American one. A more plausible aim is a strictly local non-alignment, the bomb protecting a possible British socialism from the unwanted interference of either the USA or the USSR. Such a scheme remains staggeringly quixotic and counter-intuitive. All other Labour enthusiasts for the 'nuclear deterrent' have been equally enthusiastic Atlanticists, and there is a practical reason for this. The 1958 Anglo-American Mutual Defence Agreement linked the British and American 'deterrents' together in such a manner that the two countries have never since been able to conduct a meaningfully independent foreign policy;

this agreement was part of the reason why de Gaulle kept the UK out of his own attempt at creating a 'third force', the EEC. Britain was not really militarily or economically capable of maintaining its position as a great, nuclear-armed power, irrespective of the 'moral leadership of the world' Bevan credited to it in the 1940s; it could only keep its lofty status at the price of being a client state in foreign policy. Could Bevan have broken this pact? It seems astoundingly unlikely, and any renegotiation of the 1958 agreement would surely have been considered a hostile act.

Where Bevan did not break with his fellow 'Bevanites' was in his conviction that only a radical form of social democracy could reinvigorate the Labour movement during the doldrums of the 1950s, and his dismissal of the more optimistic visions of tamed, socialised capitalism, both on principle and in terms of historical likelihood. It's common to oppose Bevan's 1952 statement of principles *In Place of Fear* to Anthony Crosland's 1956 *The Future of Socialism* as contrasting visions of what post-war social democracy could be. Although Crosland has been celebrated as a proto-Blairite, it is Bevan's account of the post-war settlement's limits that has been warranted by the experience of neoliberalism. Bevan's repeated insistence on the ultimately unreformed nature of post-war capitalism found plenty of vindication from 1974 onwards. His final Labour Conference speech, given in 1959, a year before his early death, fiercely attacks the notion that the advent of affluence has changed everything. 'Are we going to send a message from this great Labour Movement, which is the father and mother of modern democracy and modern

socialism, that we in Blackpool in 1959 have turned our
backs on our principles because of a temporary unpopular-
ity in a temporarily affluent society?' For people in Ebbw
Vale and Tredegar, Bevan's constituency, this affluence
proved to have been temporary by the 1980s, and has not
been seen since. Crosland, by contrast, honestly believed in
the 1950s that the problem of unemployment was defeated
for good. Since 1979, the jobless figure has never gone
below its then shocking, 'return to the '30s' rate of around
1.5 million, with Bevan's old stomping grounds being especially hard-hit.

In that valedictory 1959 speech, Bevan declares: 'When
they have got over the delirium of the television, when they
realise that the new homes that they have been put into are
mortgaged to the hilt, when they realise that the money-
lender has been elevated into the highest position in the
land, when they realise that [this] is a vulgar society of which
no decent person could be proud', and that this society is
'unable to exploit the resources of their scientists because
they are prevented by the greed of their capitalism from
doing so', they will find that 'the challenge of modern times'
can only be met by socialism, that, in fact, 'we represent the
future'.[49] They didn't, as it turned out, but Bevan, at least,
did represent a more attractive future than the one we now
live in. That's why Bevan remains a cult figure for a longing,
disempowered left, and Herbert Morrison does not.

One faintly disturbing thought, for those who think that
radical politics and architecture can and should go together,
emerges from this. The National Health Service has never
been a major patron of architecture. There is not a single

listed NHS hospital. Architecturally, we find a few of minor note by the large modernist firms like Yorke, Rosenberg and Mardall or Powell and Moya, and there's the odd brutalist outlier like Hampstead's monumental Royal Free; but, even before they faced heavy alteration and part-privatisation under Blair, Brown and Cameron, the actual aesthetics of NHS hospitals have been secondary, to put it mildly. It is telling that the most architecturally famous Health Centre in the country, at Finsbury, was a precursor to the NHS, not an actual product of it. This situation is a consequence of the fact that most hospitals have been built in two eras of severe cost-cutting and driving down of building standards – under Harold Wilson, and much more so, under New Labour's Private Finance Initiative. Bevan, as we've seen, did his best to commission housing that was aesthetically ambitious and pleasing. But the NHS, unlike the Festival of Britain or the modernist housing project, is something overwhelmingly admired as a system, an institution, not as something you can easily commodify. The fact that most council housing is more elegant than most NHS hospitals and health centres has had little effect on their relative esteem in the eyes of the public. Even as an economic entity, the health service has proven more difficult to privatise, needing complex, flagrantly dubious contractual wrangling and opaque devices of part-ownership to make it feasible. The institution Bevan built, and even his attempts to escape the logic of the Cold War, are examples of the limits of 1945. They are also evidence that the less obviously 'tangible' and aesthetic the political institution, the better it can potentially endure.

5

Building the Austerity City

In domestic architecture we again find exactly the same extreme specialisation which is characteristic of clothing. First there is the differentiating of quarters, which owes its origin to early London's being an agglomeration of small towns. ... To cross a street separating two quarters may mean crossing from one world into another. It is the boundary of two civilisations, two languages, two standards of life. ... The fact that the inhabitants are distributed in quarters according to their class and income has made it possible to standardise the domestic houses: as people living in the same street have the same requirements all the houses can be absolutely uniform. The uniformity of the houses is a matter of course and has not been forced upon them.

Steen Eiler Rasmussen, *London: The Unique City* (1934)[1]

The Aspirational Buy-to-Let Non-Dom Neo-Brutalist Investment Opportunity

There is a street corner in South-East London that encompasses at a glance the differences in attitude and execution in the built environment between New Labour and the 2010–15 Coalition government. On the one side is something called The Heart of East Greenwich, designed in 2006 by MAKE. This firm of former employees of Norman Foster is headed by Ken Shuttleworth, one of the head designers of the St Mary Axe 'Gherkin', that architectural emblem of the Blair years. The East Greenwich scheme was planned for the site of the former Greenwich District Hospital, a large, brutalist affair demolished in 2006–07, in one of the hugely costly PFI deals. The Heart of East Greenwich would furnish this site with three huge, twisted, gestural blocks of flats, their concrete frames clad in blue and yellow Trespa, wood panelling, and lots of metal, swooping around to define a series of 'streets' and public squares; a small health centre would be included to replace the one that had gone. Most of the scheme was, of course, designated as private housing on offer for large quantities of money; there were also plans for the usual legally mandated percentage of 'affordable' housing (the current legal definition of 'affordable' is 80 percent of market rate, which for London's working and much of its middle class is not remotely affordable). By the summer of 2015, the project was limping towards completion, with a Sainsbury's in the ground floor, but still a building site.

Just opposite is a scheme called The Peltons, designed by the much less well-known RMA Architects. This was begun in 2014, on a chaotic site around two-thirds the size of The Heart of East Greenwich, made up of wasteland, billboards, and a small, shabby shop of sign-makers. It was finished by early 2015, and it consists of a curved wall of

brick-clad flats, with completely regular, grid-like fenestration to the main road, Blackwall Lane, while to the
smaller-scale streets behind, leading to the Pelton Arms (a
popular pub from which it borrows its name) it becomes a
modernised Georgian terrace.

The contrast between the two sites couldn't be greater.
First, the gestural heroics of the 'Heart', with its deliberately
complex geometry and shiny, industrially manufactured
cladding materials, is the polar opposite of the laconic,
'vernacular' look of The Peltons. The latter, though not
particularly architecturally ambitious, immediately harmo-
nised with everything around it. It followed the street line,
with no gating or fancy forms of entry; its scale and materials blended almost imperceptibly with the architectural
styles all around, which are dominated by Georgian/early-
Victorian stock-brick classical terraces, interwar stock-brick
moderne council flats, and post-war Festival-style council
flats, with stock-brick and weatherboarded facades.

The Heart of East Greenwich

The Peltons

The lightning speed with which it was built and inhabited when compared with the 'Heart' tells its own story. However, both 'do' exactly the same thing. Both offer staggeringly expensive property to the eager parade of investors, and both of them used the fig leaf of the 'affordable' percentage to ram the project past the planning committees of the local authority.

Yet what differentiates the two sites most clearly is the rhetoric utilised to get the job done. The journeys I regularly take from south-east to central London, by train, by DLR or by bus, have always been a good place to watch 'regeneration' at work. Entire districts that didn't previously exist – 'Greenwich Central' on Creek Road in Deptford and other such geographical improbabilities – arise without fanfare. Creeks, canals and streets previously defined by strung-out light industry or GLC estates are replaced, first with concrete frames, then massive (but 'broken-up' and demonstratively irregular) blocks of flats, covered in all manner of generalised stuff – Trespa panels, aluminium balconies, swooping roofs, slatted wood.

Anyone who has been to any British city in the last decade will be familiar with the genre. This is the architecture of 'regeneration', bright, shiny, optimistic and often, despite clumsy local 'references', in sharp contrast with the existing built environment, usually being much more bulky, brightly coloured and artificial in its materials. These blocks, barging in their dozens across the inner cities of Manchester and Leeds and along the former docks of London, Leith and Liverpool, are the inescapable face of the 'urban renaissance' promised under New Labour, their privacy and expense (in terms of purchase price, not of materials) proof of its commitment to inequality. Lately, the same concrete frames have gone up, in much the same ex-industrial places, to the same six or eight storeys, and with more or less the same cram-as-many-units-in-as-possible philosophy. But that chaos of krazee clashing materials is gone, and in its place comes a new coating of traditional London stock brick. London has a new typology: the austere luxury flat, the tasteful 50s-style modernist non-dom investment.

The first real test for the style, a few years before it quietly swept the capital before it, was Accordia – a housing scheme in Cambridge designed mostly by Feilden Clegg Bradley and Alison Brooks, on former Ministry of Defence land, that won the Stirling Prize in 2008. A dense series of low-rise blocks of flats and houses, it was conspicuous for its discretion – favouring regularity of profile, repetition in silhouette, and cladding with the rough, crumbly, yellow stock brick that would become so ubiquitous. Accordia would soon reveal itself as the new orthodoxy. However, at first it appeared more as a late survival of an older Oxbridge orthodoxy, the mild vernacular modernism displayed in the work of Casson and Conder, Colin St John Wilson and Leslie Martin. Martin's Harvey Court in Cambridge and Bodleian Law Library in Oxford were particularly notable for their stock brick and strongly modelled, blocky shapes. It was ironic that this sort of self-effacing, urbane, ostentatiously contextual if slightly hair-shirted architecture was favoured in one of the most privileged and pampered parts of the country. However, the 'Cambridge style' had quickly been drowned out by the more strident modernism of brutalism and high-tech, and even more so by the shrill, flippant historicism of postmodern architecture. Aside from one large-scale example, Colin St John Wilson's British Library, this is not one of the dominant styles of twentieth-century British architecture, which made its sudden return in 2008 all the more surprising.

The designers of Accordia have, atypically for an architecture firm, had a lot more work *since* the financial crisis. But the most unexpectedly successful firm of the last few years is Maccreanor Lavington, who had hitherto specialised in housing schemes in the Netherlands, where much higher standards of rectitude and material are demanded by town planners and local authorities than pertain in England. Somehow, since 2010 they have become arguably the defining architecture firm of contemporary London, leading huge projects at King's Cross and the Royal Docks, where schemes that would once have been gussied up with attention-grabbing tat have emerged instead as unbroken expanses of brick. Like most regeneration schemes, a lot depends on where the money's going; so, at the large luxury housing estate in King's Cross, the quality of materials is extremely high. To anyone used to the way that contemporary London architecture since the late 1990s has felt intangible, tinny, tacky, afraid of physicality and permanence and any sort of urban order, it is bracing to visit these clusters of towers on the Regent's Canal. Suddenly, various qualities long missing from the city's housing – rhythm, regularity, shade, moulding, a sense of weight and depth – *presence*, in short – are deployed on a grand scale. What is perhaps even more impressive, though, is the fact that the reason for this concern with physical surface may be much the same as that which motivated the previous use of wood-effect Trespa and multicoloured panels. The architecture of, say, the housing and office blocks of Salford Quays utilises clashing materials, wavy roofs and

Flagship of the new London vernacular: Kings Cross Central

multiple heights as a way of distracting the eye from the sheer volume of the lettable space; and something similar is happening here. When you look at the blocks of the new King's Cross, your eye is drawn by the surfaces – the intricate, rhythmic moulding, the tactile surfaces of the detailed brickwork, the seemingly natural warmth of the colours. Seen from a distance, though, you realise that these towers are as ultra-dense as any scheme by MAKE or their ilk, and similarly attempt to mask that density through various kinds of display and contortion, pulling themselves into craggy shapes and skylines so as to humanise the dogged filling of as many inches of the site as possible.

This is more obvious at the lesser scheme in the Royal Docks, where the budget hasn't stretched to the expressionistic modelling used so interestingly at King's Cross, and you have instead just some unusually well-clad yuppie flats. Many more projects along these lines are now rising from almost every major gap site in the capital. Their qualities are particularly evident when seen side by side with earlier, crasser conceptions of how to sell luxury – as at Canada Water, where Glenn Howells's new housing uses its brick panels as a screen against the fibreglass domes and gold griddles used in the nearby work of CZWG. Cladding here is a serious business. So serious, in fact, that it may have played a role in the brick shortage which beset the London building industry a couple of years ago.

This can have strange consequences. The entire point, I had assumed, of the multi-clad, behatted Trespa pseudomodernism of the New Labour era was that it was 'aspirational'. It was the opposite of austerity in its aesthetic – it was hierarchical, high-tech, futuristic, bright to the point of being garish. The reason for this was that it needed to sell *separateness*. Most of the urban schemes of that time were placed in council estates, former industrial estates, formerly working canals and docksides – areas that have long had a bad reputation, or could be considered 'edgy'. Something had to be done in terms of architecture to make abundantly clear to buyers and investors that this was not poor people's housing.

Now, something like Maccreanor Lavington's work in King's Cross, or a far lesser example such as The Peltons, has some similarities with the typology that has been the most cherished in London since the 1970s – the regular, brick-clad, rectilinear Georgian terrace. More surprisingly, these schemes also have much in common with the regularity, monumentality and order of post-war housing estates, particularly in their use of square, bricky towers. In fact, they come across as a surprising reconciliation of these two moments of metropolitan good taste, merging the spec builder with the local authority. Rather than being opposed, this is the unity of the aesthetics of Cubitt's, the spec builders that designed and constructed most of inner London in the early nineteenth century, and the London County Council, which built most of the rest between the 1930s and the 1960s.

It is hard to object to this on purely architectural grounds. The simple fact is that London's new housing in 2015 is flatly superior to London's new housing in 2005, in terms of the relation of buildings to their neighbours, in the quality of materials, and often, even in terms of the size of rooms and the provision of balconies. One reason for this is the abandonment of the obsessive differentiation between Regeneration and the presumed Degeneration all around it that marked New Labour architecture. This architecture is not embarrassed to be where it is. However, it can lead to some strange moments. I was surprised one afternoon to find in the free Boris Johnson propaganda and property porn rag, the *Evening Standard*, an advertisement for a new stunning development somewhere in Clapham where the old imagery of white pyjamas, glasses of wine and magnificent views of glistening skyscrapers coexisted happily with this bricky Cambridge-style modernism, which I'd previously associated with beardy lecturers and owners of architecture monographs. How did that happen?

The new London brick phenomenon is ultimately the result of a London Design Guide published by the mayor of London, the very same Boris Johnson, in 2009. As sympathetic observers David Birkbeck and Julian Hart note in their brochure on this 'New London Vernacular', 'the principal driver' of this 'convergence' of flats and houses, social and 'high-end residential', has been 'the direction of the London Mayor's design guide'. The guide's demand for an 'obvious point of entry' from the street to the front door has 'pushed architects to borrow from London's stock of terraced houses'. As a result, 'a riot of one-off statement buildings is giving way to this restrained architecture of a few common details',[2] and, in a shift to a different, non-architectural language, 'the discrete organisation of accommodation offers a low-risk solution for mix and management'.

The mayor's design guidelines did not, of course, mandate a legally binding return to regular fenestration and brick cladding, although they did place great stress on that floating signifier, 'context'. They mandated various things which actually seem fairly laudable – flats should be double aspect, should have decently sized balconies, they should have clear entrances, rather than obscure doors placed behind gates, and they should be no smaller than the 'Parker-Morris' dimensions established as the legal minimum for public housing in the early 1960s. Also, the 'mix', in housing divided between market, affordable and (occasionally) social was to be 'tenure-blind', that is, without obvious divides between the various types: a rule that is still, in reality, honoured mostly in the breach.

'The market' did the rest. Or rather, 'it' chose brick, terraces and clearly defined towers on clear street lines because these features, to quote the authors of *A New London Vernacular* again, 'reduce sales risk', 'reduce design and construction risk' and 'enable more accurate land valuation'. In other words, building brick homes and marketing them is easy to do, and became a safe option after the financial crisis. This was no time for any more experiments. In addition, the new vernacular resembled the post-war council flat that had ceased to be demonised after many of its products were rehabilitated by the austerity nostalgia industry. This was partly (*mea culpa*) because defences in books and articles had made them more acceptable to middle-class aesthetes. Crucially, though, via the effects of government inducements to Right to Buy and Buy to Let, ex-council flats were easily obtained by developers, then marketed and sold and rented to middle-class professionals. In terms of their space standards, storage, views and style, the cream of this stock was among the best housing in London. After the initial shock of being asked for so much moolah for a council flat in Bethnal Green, buyers came to realise they were actually buying something far superior to expectations.

So what emerges particularly clearly from all of this is that austerity – in terms here of developers and investors wanting safety and predictability – has pushed much of the very fabric of London towards an austerity-nostalgic aesthetic. Whereas in very recent memory, London seemed to want to look like Dubai-on-Thames, it now increasingly resembles a cross between Islington in the 1820s and Poplar in the 1950s, two moments of austerity and rectitude. It shows that while local government seems to have no ability or desire to influence *what* developers build, it is able to influence how they clad it. Boris Johnson hasn't the power and certainly hasn't the will to build thousands of new council flats in London, but what he and his administration have managed to do is help developers build thousands of luxury flats which look like council flats, and can appear to be 'in keeping' with them. Some may still hanker for the more traditional aesthetics of luxury – floor-to-ceiling windows, metallic balconies, white walls and what have you – but in a city with so captive a market as this, those investors who are not enthused by the new vernacular are presumably not too put off by the replacement of the barcode facade with the brick panel, given that their profit margins will remain spectacular.

However, it is taking critics some time to notice that the aesthetic of London today, at the nadir of its housing crisis, at the moment where the gap between rich and poor is wider than at any time since the 1930s, is no longer the plutocratic cacophony of St George's Wharf or Stratford High Street. It's sober, well-mannered, increasingly well-made. As if the response to the housing crisis was to make housing for the privileged less conspicuous, less of an aggressive imposition on the eyes of the unprivileged. This aesthetic says, 'Look, we live in normal brick houses, just like you.'

Firebomb Classicism

On the anniversary of the 7 July 2004 bombings in London, the monument to the event by architects Carmody Groarke was defaced. The designers had used a minimalist language that is increasingly familiar – clusters of thin steel stelae, one for each victim, are placed in four corners for the London locations of the attacks. After the defacement, spray-painted stencils ran vertically along each of them – it looked as if they were made to measure. The messages were of such *Four Lions*–like idiocy – 'J7 Truth', 'Four Innocent Muslims' – that the attack was obviously motivated by impressive political moronism. However, in the process, this scrupulously mute memorial suddenly had a domineering voice baying all over it, interpreting its architecture not as an abstract empty space, but as a blank canvas to be written upon.

There has been a minor rash of new memorials in London over the past decade, moving in tandem with, first, the vaulting forms of MAKE and their ilk, and then feeling much more comfortable with the new Georgian-LCC style of the austerity years. There have been figurative statues, viz. the clumsy effigies of everyone from Lloyd George to Bobby Charlton built in the last couple of decades. And there have been classical commemorative complexes: the memorial to the Women of World War II, on Whitehall, where uniforms in bronze bulge out from a vaguely Lutyensesque plinth. There's the more comic Animals in War, caught on the patch of grass between Park Lane and Hyde Park, where creatures unaware of the world-historical events they're participating in peer at us haplessly and plaintively.

The biggest of them all is the Bomber Command memorial just off Green Park, funded by the Conservative grandee Lord Ashcroft. As the historian Gavin Stamp pointed out with some disgust when making it his 'worst building of 2014' in *Private Eye*, the plaque honouring the donor is as large as those honouring the dead. Like so much of what passes for classical architecture in the UK, the structure manages to be both precious and pompous at the same time. The Memorial itself immortalises a force which is, to say the least, controversial for its role in the massacres of defenceless civilians in Dresden, Cologne, Hamburg and elsewhere (though an easily missed inscription tells us it's for their victims, too), with a prissy, thin, ill-proportioned set of Disneyland Doric columns around a central group of realistic figures. This is the outright Tory version of the new austerity aesthetic, tailored seemingly to the most outright reactionary prejudices. It is as if the war memorials

The temple to Bomber Command

we have already were too unnerving, too violent or too abstract, so they had to be replaced with something friendlier. A short walk from the gormless Bomber Command monument are memorials of far greater power by Edwin Lutyens and C. S. Jagger, but they will not do; the aesthetics of 1918 are now too radical for us. Best plant the moat of the Tower of London with poppies instead.

These are examples of monuments to wars about which – almost – everyone already knows what they think; hence the cloying literalism that currently proliferates. Abstraction, on the other hand, tends to be deployed when an event is still raw, still able to upset people, open to interpretation in different ways. It was well used by one of the more interesting Benevolent Bureaucracies of the interwar years, the Imperial War Graves Commission. In the aftermath of World War I, architects such as Edwin Lutyens and Charles Holden were commissioned to design memorials of unusual originality and sensitivity. As outlined in Stamp's own recent book on Lutyens's *Memorial to the Missing of the Somme*, in Thiepval, northern France, the War Graves Commission, for all its imperialism, had tried to move away from a tradition favouring victory and vainglory in favour of some acknowledgement, however tacit, of the pointlessness of suffering. To commemorate the unfound bodies of the Somme, Lutyens designed an arch of loss, not of triumph – what triumph was there to celebrate? Again, with the Cenotaph in Whitehall, Lutyens managed, impressively, to resist widespread calls for Christian imagery – what about the Jewish, Hindu or Muslim dead, he pointed out – and for any obvious representational sculpture, the lamenting angels and so on that were standard for the genre. Instead he designed a delicate yet imposing Portland stone plinth, saying nothing except 'OUR GLORIOUS DEAD' – the second word was as near he got to triumphalism – and topped by a stone wreath. It effectively suggested that something horrible and unprecedented had happened, which couldn't be dealt with in the old way.

Stamp would probably argue that the difference between Lutyens's memorial and Carmody Groarke's memorial to 7/7 is that the former still has some affinity with a familiar language, a continuity with the classical architecture of death. The complex tapering proportions, the heavy stone, the wreath become, in the second example, reduced to the banality of simple steel girders. They suggest the language not of classicism – the building as a 'finished' object – but of industry, where buildings are semi-provisional. Yet like Lutyens's memorials, the 7/7 memorial avoids sentimentality, condescension, pomposity or moralism. It, too, 'looks like a memorial', and is essentially familiar. As in Peter Eisenman's Memorial to the Murdered Jews of Europe, in Berlin, the freedom of interpretation coincides with a freedom of space, where shapes demarcate an unprogrammed emptiness. Visit the Holocaust memorial to see it used by children as a particularly fiendish maze.

One World War I memorial, not far from the 7/7 sculptures, suggests what a 'speaking' memorial could be – the Royal Artillery memorial, sculpted by C. S. Jagger. Its Portland stone machine guns and hooded-eyed, beaten-down figures do not come across as misplaced or kitsch, but profoundly disturbing. Of all the many memorials in the area it is the least easy to walk past unthinkingly – as soon as you notice it, you're captivated by its intensity and sense of horror, shaken up. It would be pointless to deface it to remind passers-by of the evils of war, as they are conveyed already.

The American architect Daniel Libeskind used to try to convey these sorts of feelings and associations via forms that would make you feel ill or uneasy, with slopes and titanium to act as a synechdoche for trench foot or shelling at the Manchester Imperial War Museum North, opposite Salford Quays. But the memorialising architecture that he and other deconstructivists specialised in during the 1990s is not terribly fashionable anymore. The favoured model of memorial space is much closer to something like Carmody Groarke's memorial than the overambitious, clashing forms of Libeskind's war museum in Dresden or Jewish Museum in Berlin, cheapened by their overuse for more prosaic functions, like students' unions and luxury flats. But while Libeskind's Imperial War Museum North now seems the product of a bygone New Labour era, the new refurbishment of the original Imperial War Museum in London by Norman Foster, opened in 2014 on the 100th anniversary of the First World War, is so spectacularly ill-judged that you almost long for Libeskind's earnestness – at least he gave the impression of actually caring about the subject matter. But exploring the refurbished museum is, at least, an instructive journey around one country's massively confused sense of its own history.

The very notion of an 'Imperial War Museum' may provoke a bit of a shudder in certain quarters. The name is bad enough. For instance, even the Imperial War Graves Commission renamed itself the Commonwealth War Graves Commission over half a century ago. The building itself has a deeply uncomfortable history, intriguingly so – beneath its sober portico and dome was previously Bethlehem Hospital, whose nickname, 'Bedlam', became a synonym for mental

Stormin Norman: the Imperial War Museum

hospitals. Inside, there's still more than a whiff of Bedlam about it. In the obligatory atrium, planes hang from cables and missiles point up at a jagged suspended ceiling, barely concealing an 80s glass dome; a baffling system of circulation leads you constantly, pointlessly up and down, with levels that look like they connect leading nowhere, and inclined walls supporting it all. The glassy, airy, business-park atrium has long been Foster's model for almost everything, from a City Academy to the British Museum to the Reichstag, but here the elegance and clarity Foster brings, at best, to this now rather tired trope has disappeared in a mess of clumsy angles.

I'm quite sure Foster will have justified this as a reaction to perhaps the most important thing about the Imperial War Museum — its collection of paintings and sculptures, whose cross-section of British artists responding to the shock and horror of their wartime experiences made, and still makes it, one of the best (and least visited) modern art galleries in Britain. The most famous possessions are the vorticist works by Wyndham Lewis, William Roberts and David Bomberg. Maybe those jagged roofs are a 'reference' to Lewis's *A Battery Shelled*, a panoramic landscape of abstracted destruction, now translated into faceted metal suspended ceilings. If so, the metaphor is rather hard to take in, as the building's much more makeshift, if much less counter-intuitive, previous refurbishment keeps poking through in the corners. The main atrium was always a faintly triumphalist collection of random big weapons under a big and cheap dome, and it is still that, plus lots of aimless circuits crammed in to make the place feel both triumphalist and claustrophobic. The effect makes it clear the architects haven't properly thought out the space, as arbitrary patterns lead up the atrium to something called the 'Lord Ashcroft Gallery' (him again). That confusion is constantly reflected in the exhibits. The art collection aside, the museum has been aimed at children for some time, but the infantilisation now feels especially extreme. Little 'post-it notes' appear next to every exhibit on the floor that outlines Britain's post-1945 military history, sketching out in the minimum of words of minimum length the minimum of information, as jollily as possible. What's more, a cursory wander round can uncover outright inaccuracies: for example, the Korean War as a battle between the 'democratic' south and the dictatorial north, when the south didn't hold fair elections until several decades after the conflict. More unsurprisingly, there is a refusal to confront anything too uncomfortable: the Troubles in Northern Ireland are presented as if the British Army was a baffled onlooker rather than an active participant, but all ends happily when Ian Paisley and Martin McGuinness open an IKEA together. Given that there's actually an exhibit specifically for children – a show about spying, based around one of the 'Horrible Histories' books – it's unclear whether this isn't really a case of talking down to adults.

All is explained, as always, in the gift shop. After you've gone pointlessly up and down a few flights of steps, two distinct shops appear. One is 'serious', and sells history books and a new catalogue with an introduction by the duke of Cambridge. The other is a great big emporium of austerity nostalgia, a place to pig out on Gill Sans, muted colours,

Blitz spirit, crown logos, wartime cooking, duplicate ration cards – whatever your fantasy about living in genuine privation and fear might be.

But really, the two are seamless. The exhibits themselves come across like a three-dimensional version of one of those books that tell you with big pictures and minimal text what it was like fighting the Hun and eating spam: narcissistic wallowing in fake poverty and barely coherent history as a way of avoiding any thought of how to drag ourselves out of our current, needless, and far less egalitarian version of austerity. The 'rationing experience' – organic wartime cuisine to be cooked in the Aga of a ruthlessly scrubbed ex-council flat. There's probably an app for it. The perpetuation of this mechanism is the real function Foster had to design for – a space that would encapsulate the conflation of austerity 1945 and austerity 2015. Having Prince William sign the foreword to the catalogue is a reminder that much of the latter austerity has revolved around Royal Spectacles, as if there was a Ministry of Royal Procreation spurring on the younger royals to offer an appropriately jingoistic distraction. Because of how cheap and flimsy it is, Foster's Imperial War Museum is maybe a more appropriate response to austerity 2015, housing the trinkets of the past (and, of course, their current reproductions) in a building that evokes a *Bravo Two Zero* version of a PFI hospital. The Museum of Keeping Calm and Carrying On.

The Embalming of Modernism

Returning, however, from this outright flag-waving to the careful cultivation of London as an austerity capital, we need to look again at the process by which modernist architecture and social democratic urban planning have become major sources for austerity nostalgia

In 1994, we found Raphael Samuel arguing that municipal modernism and its emblem in the UK, the council estate, was the inverse of heritage culture; the two were, he proposed, irreconcilable enemies. In order for this type of modernism to become part of the economy again, that is, for it to generate speculative profits, it had first to become absorbed into heritage. For this to occur, an outright physical evisceration was necessary.

The first major modernist structure in the UK to go through a simultaneous restoration and change in its function was Keeling House, a 'cluster block' of council housing in Bethnal Green, in the East End of London, designed in the late 1950s by Denys Lasdun and restored by Munkenbeck & Marshall in 1998. The spalled concrete of this experimental tower – one which tried in its layout to preserve some of the aspects of working-class communality apparently found in the terraced houses it replaced – meant that it became prohibitively expensive for Tower Hamlets Council to maintain, particularly after the building was listed by English Heritage for its architectural significance. It was sold at a pittance to property developers, who paid for its restoration, built a penthouse on top, gated the whole thing from the still shabby streets around, and made a killing. With this precedent, the various 'iconic' but

The iconic Keeling House

local authority-owned blocks of inner London were suddenly fair game for property developers, who had scarcely ventured into this territory before.

The more incremental, 'organic' form of this took absorption of municipal modernism into heritage via the Right to Buy. A council tenant, or someone who bought from someone who bought from someone who was once a council tenant, could now make a packet from the sale of their flat (which they had, of course, bought at discount, with most of the money going straight to the treasury rather than to the local authority who built the thing). Because of this, a flat in a particularly 'iconic' block by a respected architect – Ernő Goldfinger's Trellick Tower (though not his earlier Balfron Tower, currently being directly sold off to rich investors) or, as we've seen, Berthold Lubetkin's Sivill House – could cost you or make you an enormous sum of money, not far from the cost of the original construction. Needless to say, when introduced in the 1980s, this policy did not please those who commissioned the buildings – 'Old Labour' councils all, committed to the provision of low-cost, high-quality housing for the working class – nor did it please the architects; both Goldfinger and Lubetkin were close fellow travellers with the Communist Party of Great Britain.

The new appreciation of the buildings, based on their quality and 'character', meant that their original purpose had to be destroyed. In many cases this meant changes to the fabric of the building, too – although very seldom in terms of the actual plan or layout, as large flats with French windows were not a difficult sell to the transnational capitalist class. The changes were mostly cosmetic: some concrete repaired, or in the case of Keeling House and London's Brunswick Centre, some painting of concrete. Even in the most drastic example – the gutting of the flats from the concrete frame of Sheffield's Park Hill estate – the building was structurally sound, and the replacement flats had a very similar spatial layout.

The irony of this is so gigantic, and so gross, that it feels almost too bloody obvious to point out, but apparently we must. In Britain today we are living through exactly the kind of housing crisis for which council housing was invented in the first place, at exactly the same time as we're alternately fetishising and privatising its remnants. From substandard speculative housing to runaway inflation of mortgages and rents, from resurrected Rachmanism to houses in garden sheds and garages, from empty flats in the north to neo-Victorian overcrowding in the south, from a forced exodus due to unemployment in one city through to a forced exodus due to house prices and rents in another, we face a massive problem for which, once, the solution was the building of well-designed, well-considered, well-planned modernist buildings, often erected on the ashes of the shoddily-designed, unplanned, badly made, profit-driven housing of the past. Instead, what is actually happening is that we're transforming the surviving fragments of that solution into one of the main contributors to the problem, as social housing becomes the new front line of gentrification, and the architect-designed modernist flat the new loft conversion.

The dialectic of obsolescence, repair and restoration has gone haywire, as need and aesthetics come into increasingly obvious conflict. Never has modernist architecture been so fulsomely commemorated. Television programmes, exhibitions, films, books, estate agents' brochures and, as we've seen, a new wave of trinkets such as plates and tea towels appeal to the modernist nostalgia that makes us gaze with proud affection at the buildings' stark and confident forms, so unlike our own contemporary efforts, alternately clumsy and egotistical (circa 2005) or timid and anal (circa 2015). And in so doing we add to a climate in which these places become ever more lucrative for developers, who will, while leaving the buildings largely alone, transform them into shells, an architecture voided of its original content – *at the very moment when it is most needed*. Many of the works that have helped modernism become part of the heritage are complicit in this to some degree. Certainly the author hasn't been guiltless in that regard; nor have such projects as 'A Clockwork Jerusalem', the British Pavilion at the Venice Architecture Biennale in 2014. Here, a series of disparate, aggressive, sometimes reformist, sometimes revolutionary moments were swept into a consensus that would have baffled George Osborne, but which you could easily imagine Jon Cruddas or Andy Burnham applauding. Blake, Morris, the Garden Cities, Cumbernauld, Thamesmead, neo-Georgian, Mock Tudor and the New Brutalism, all yoked to the same project of urban-rural arcadia. All of us wanted to Build Jerusalem in this Green and Pleasant Land.

In the exhibition's central image, a crescent was composed of Stonehenge, Bath's Royal Crescent and the Hulme housing estate in Manchester, with the mound from Alison and Peter Smithson's condemned Robin Hood Gardens estate in the middle: a striking image of continuity that would have seemed deeply subversive in the 1980s, but which now feels deeply consensual. The only passing nod to any post-utopian use of council estates was a flyer for a party in Hulme in the late 1980s. It goes without saying that any glimpses of those who actually live in the housing estates and new towns was conspicuous by its absence.

The Anti-Melancholic City

That absence is common to a great deal of austerity-nostalgic depictions of urban space. You'll search in vain for the people that actually live in most housing estates on the various 'I Heart Brutalism' Tumblr post, where any picture not taken in black and white in 1972 is excised. You'll struggle to find much more than lip service to the fact of urban Britain's huge racial and cultural diversity in the literature of 'progressive patriotism', except in the likes of *The New East End*, where it is mentioned only as a way of contrasting the work ethic of the common Eastender with the sense of entitlement of the Bengali migrant. *The Spirit of '45* is based on forgetting what happened in 1948, reliving instead an unrepeatable moment of cohesion. The Empire vanishes, and so do the descendants of its subjects. Every part of this new aesthetic cherry-picked from a pre-pop era is also, frankly, a whiting-out, where the syncretic cultures that developed here from the 1950s onwards disappear. Presumably, they're tainted by the fact that they developed even after the Fall, or the election of Margaret Thatcher as we prefer to call it. The urbanism of ostentatious cohesion and unified frontages, the Farrow & Ball world of good taste and stock brick, is one that is at the very least implicitly exclusive.

I can't help thinking that a city that is *not* melancholic, that is *not* based on either an austerity that coexists with an ever more obscenely rich 1 percent, *nor* a 'social democracy of fear', is the best we can hope for. Paul Gilroy's *After Empire* contrasted the 'post-colonial melancholia' of the Blitz Spirit and the alleged failure of multiculturalism with the 'conviviality' of the really existing multicultural city, which, however pressured it currently is, remains an achievement that simply cannot be explained by the persistence of the Spirit of 1945. Gilroy's examples of convivial culture are musical or comic, but in some ways, this conviviality has irrupted into politics in the last five years. While thousands may have watched poverty porn on

TV, the people of Derby Road in Southampton banded together to refuse to take part in *Immigration Street*. In 2011, the marchers on the demonstrations against the education reforms were London youth infuriated as much by the abolition of the Education Maintenance Allowance as by the trebling of university tuition fees. In the last year, the 'Focus E15 Mums' of the London Borough of Newham occupied disused council flats, otherwise fit only for gentrification or demolition. These people have not shown the Blitz Spirit, they have not kept their upper lips stiff, they have not kept calm or carried on, and their iconography and slogans reflect that.

When Focus E15 Mums took over the disused but structurally sound (even recently renovated) Carpenters Estate in Stratford, in the shadow of new austerity-chic blocks of flats, or when squatters occupied the huge, system-built Aylesbury Estate in Peckham, they did not demand that the buildings be used because they're part of the great history

'These homes need people, these people need homes'

of British democracy, nor because they were precious remnants of a welfare state, and least of all because they thought they were great examples of the *architecture* of the welfare state. They took them over and tried to use them because they are useful, and nostalgia played absolutely no part in their actions.

These are the true defenders of the welfare state, not those who would tell us tales of the old working-class communities, of the unbroken line connecting sensible Mr Attlee, Magna Carta and the free-born Englishman; not those who would tear the brief, aberrant achievements of social democracy out of their historically untypical context and flog them as another great moment in our heritage. If a social and democratic city is going to be built again, it will most probably be built by those who have no investment in the past, no fond memory of it. That isn't to say they'll be building on nothing. There is something to conserve, Tony Judt was right about that much – the very fact a publicly owned Carpenters Estate existed at all was the reason why it sat empty, and the reason why the slogan of the young mothers who occupied it could be so clear and so practical: 'These people need homes, these homes need people.' Such words are unlikely to find their way into white letters on a red poster, with an emblem of the crown above them. If we're ever going to escape from austerity, this clear statement of collective utility is the most likely way out.

Acknowledgements

This short book derives originally from an article published in 2009 in *Radical Philosophy*, 'Lash Out and Cover Up', which in turn derived from a post on the blog *Sit Down Man, You're a Bloody Tragedy*. Thanks to Esther Leslie for making me write it up into something coherent, and to Leo Hollis and Rowan Wilson at Verso for letting me do so in book form. Any coherence at this greater length, if it exists, is owed to the rearrangements insisted on by Leo, and to Lorna Scott Fox's forensic copyediting. Small parts derive from articles for the *London Review of Books*, *Dezeen* and the *Guardian*; thanks to Paul Myerscough, Anna Winston, Stephen Moss and Natalie Hanman for commissioning them. Some fragments have also evolved from an essay written for the book supplementing Luke Fowler's *The Poor Stockinger, the Luddite Cropper and the Deluded Followers of Joanna Southcott* (Film and Video Umbrella, 2014), with thanks to Steven Bode and Luke Fowler.

The following all helped me with ideas, for the most part unwittingly and hence cannot be blamed for any of it: Fatema Ahmed, Scott Anthony, Henderson Downing, Tom Gann, Joe Kennedy, Richard King, Huw Lemmey, Victoria McNeile, Carl Neville, Alex Niven, Daniel Trilling, Will Wiles. In particular, love and gratitude is due to Agata Pyzik, for bearing with England and all it has entailed since 2010.

Notes

Introduction

1   See loonyparty.com/history-4, accessed 11 May 2015.

2   For an argument that this escape into a pre-60s form of asexuality was a protest against the oppressive 'fitness' of 80s sexual politics, see Simon Reynolds, 'Against Health and Efficiency', in Angela McRobbie, ed., *Zoot Suits and Second-Hand Dresses* (Harper Collins, 1988). However, the current moment is a rather different one – unlike the 'cutie' look of mid-80s refuse-niks, the nouveau-austerity look for men (tattoos, beards) and women (red lipstick, cleavage) is as starkly gendered as that of, say, contemporary hip hop.

3   Raphael Samuel, *Theatres of Memory: Past and Present in Contemporary Culture* (Verso, 2012), p. 113.

4   Ibid., p. 111.

5   Ibid., p. 163.

6   Patrick Wright, *On Living in an Old Country* (Verso, 1985), p. 46.

7   Ibid., pp. 155–6.

1. Lash Out and Cover Up

1   In George Orwell, *The Collected Essays, Journalism and Letters, vol. 2: My Country Right or Left* (Penguin, 1970), pp. 503–4.

2   Paul Gilroy, *After Empire: Melancholia or Convivial Culture?* (Routledge, 2004), pp. 96–7.

3   Douglas Coupland, *Generation X: Tales for an Accelerated Culture* (Abacus, 1997), p. 47.

4   See the 'official' website of this copyright-free image, at keepcalmand-carryon.com/history/. It also usefully features a link to a 1997 academic dissertation on the subject – 'The Planning, Design and Reception of British Home Front Propaganda Posters during the Second World War', by Bex Lewis, who notes that Herbert Morrison's slogan 'GO TO IT!' was a far more popular poster at the time. It was not in a sober sans serif, and featured no crown. See drbexl.co.uk/1997/05/the-first-posters/, and from her thesis, on Keep Calm … itself, drbexl.co.uk/2009/04/the-original-history-of-keep-calm-and-carry-on-phd-extract/, accessed 11 May 2015.

5   Tom Gardner, 'Jamie Oliver's Ministry of Food is closed by inspectors for "welfare and safety"', *Daily Mail*, 28 June 2013.

6   From their website at canteen.co.uk, accessed 11 May 2015.

7   All quotes from itunes.apple.com/us/app/rationbook, accessed 11 May 2015.

8   Simon Reynolds, 'Society of the Spectral', *The Wire*, November 2006.

9   For a defence of these ideas, see Mark Fisher's *Ghosts of My Life* (Zero, 2014).

10   For a sympathetic critique of this 'hauntological' music as a form of recondite, ultra-clever alternative history-making, see Simon Reynolds, *Retromania: Pop Culture's Addiction to Its Own Past* (Faber, 2011). Reynolds perspicaciously notes that all of the references made by these groups are about circumventing and avoiding the very familiar narrative of pop, where the public culture of social democracy or 'Butskellism', with its focus on education, the public sphere, 'Apollonian' modern architecture and town planning and the collective over the individual are re-imagined not as oppressive, but as potentially liberatory – which in the context of a rampant neoliberalism administered by people who grew up on pop, they certainly seem to be. But of course neoliberalism can assimilate this aesthetic as much as it can any other.

11   Gary Mills, 'Giving up the Ghost', *Dodgem Logic* 8, Spring 2011.

2. Can the Ghost of Clement Attlee Save Us?

1   Tony Benn, *Years of Hope: Diaries, Papers and Letters, 1940–1962* (Arrow, 1994), p. 90.

2   This is an interesting reversal. Cf: 'When the Beveridge Report was published, it had to be somewhat soft-pedalled in the news bulletins to India. There was danger that it would cause serious resentment, the likeliest Indian reaction being: "They are making themselves comfortable at our expense."' George Orwell, 'London Letter to *Partisan Review*, August 1945', in *The Collected Essays, Journalism and Letters, Vol. 3*, p. 449.

3   Among the several critiques of the film on this basis, see Anna Chen, 'People of colour like me have been painted out of working-class history', *Guardian*, 16 July 2013.

4   Simon Garfield, *Our Hidden Lives* (Ebury Press, 2004), p. 17.

5   Perry Anderson, 'The Myths of Edward Thompson', *New Left Review* 135, 1966.

6   E. P. Thompson, 'Homage to Tom Maguire', in *Making History* (New Press, 1995), p. 24.

7   For a short film focusing just on these, see Matthew Tempest's *Building Societies* (2014).

3. The Aesthetic Empire of Ingsoc

1   J. M. Richards, *Modern Architecture* (Pelican, 1953), p. 99.

2   Lindsay Bagshaw, 'Romantic Moderns', *The Chap*, February–March 2011.

3   Alexandra Harris, *Romantic Moderns: English Writers, Artists and the Imagination from Virginia Woolf to John Piper* (Thames and Hudson, 2015), p. 10.

4   Ibid., p. 48.

5   Ibid., p. 206.

6   Ibid., p. 247.

7   Ibid., p. 271.

8   Ibid., p. 267.

9   Ibid., p. 252.

10   J. B. Priestley, *English Journey* (Penguin, 1977), p. 10.

11   Ibid., p. 375.

12 Jonathan Glancey, *London: Bread and Circuses* (Verso, 2003), p. 12.

13 Ibid., p. 30.

14 Ibid., p. 38.

15 Michael T. Saler, *The Avant-Garde in Interwar England: Medieval Modernism and the London Underground* (Oxford University Press, 1999), p. 28.

16 Quoted in Oliver Green, *Frank Pick's London: Art, Design and the Modern City* (V&A, 2013), p. 15.

17 On Yerkes's impressive achievements and his equally impressive dodginess, see Christian Wolmar, *The Subterranean Railway* (Atlantic, 2004), pp. 161–92.

18 Nikolaus Pevsner, *The Buildings of England: Middlesex* (Penguin, 1951), p. 26.

19 Richards, *Modern Architecture*, pp. 99–100.

20 These posters can be found in David Bownes and Oliver Green, eds, *London Transport Posters: A Century of Art and Design* (Lund Humphries, 2008), which also includes some useful critical essays which I have drawn on here to some extent.

21 Quoted in Scott Anthony, *Public Relations and the Making of Modern Britain: Stephen Tallents and the Birth of a Progressive Media Profession* (Manchester University Press, 2012), p. 26.

22 Saler, *Avant-Garde in Interwar England*, p. 121.

23 Albert Speer, who would know, claimed that the nondescript, Edwardian-classical Whiteley's department store in Kensington was Hitler's favoured headquarters. See Edward Jones and Christopher Woodward, *A Guide to the Architecture of London* (Phoenix, 2013), p. 178.

24 Quoted in Bernard Semmel, *Imperialism and Social Reform: British Social Imperial Thought, 1895–1914* (Anchor, 1968), p. 174.

25 Ibid., p. 176.

26 Quoted in ibid., p. 223.

27 Ibid., p. 218.

28 Tellingly, a typical austerity-nostalgia product like *E. McKnight Kauffer: Design* (Antique Collectors Club, 2007), one of a series encompassing the likes of Paul Nash, Abram Games and Eric Ravilious, features not a single example of Kauffer's many posters for the EMB. Similarly, *Frank Pick's London* manages to include one EMB poster from the scores Pick commissioned – and that one is of an English car factory!

29   Pick, quoted in Cathy Ross, *Twenties London: A City in the Jazz Age* (Philip Wilson, 2003), p. 82.

30   Ibid., pp. 68–9.

31   Anthony, *Public Relations*, p. 114.

32   Ibid., p. 7.

33   Ibid., p. 44.

34   Stephen Tallents, *The Production of England* (1932), reproduced as an appendix to Anthony, *Public Relations*, p. 222.

35   Quoted in the typically extensive programme notes for the BFI's *Land of Promise: The British Documentary Movement* (BFI, 2009), p. 28.

36   Scott Anthony, *Night Mail* (BFI, 2007), p. 41.

4. Family Portrait

1   Quoted in Michael Foot, *Aneurin Bevan, 1897–1960* (Indigo, 1997), pp. 589–90.

2   Tom Harrisson, *Living through the Blitz* (Penguin, 1990), p. 37.

3   Ibid., p. 62.

4   Ibid., p. 152.

5   Ibid., p. 157.

6   Ibid., p. 162.

7   Ibid., p. 326.

8   Ibid., p. 240.

9   Ibid., p. 82.

10   Ibid., p. 85.

11   Ibid., p. 247.

12   Ibid., p. 177.

13   Ibid., p. 293.

14   The pair had donated money to the 44 Group, an anti-fascist street-fighting group based in London's East End.

15   Bringing us back to the evasive subject matter of *God's Chillun*, the Trinidadian Trotskyist historian C. L. R James used the family metaphor in the late 1930s to describe how European imperialism produced the modern Caribbean: 'Every succeeding year ... saw the labouring population, slave or free, incorporating into itself more and more of the language, customs, aims and outlook of its masters. It steadily grew in numbers until it became a terrifying majority of the population. The ruling minority therefore was in the

position of the father who produced children and had to guard against being supplanted by them.'

In this reading, the Empire really was a 'family', and one whose problems could only end by the slaying of its singularly brutal patriarch. James, *The Black Jacobins* (Vintage, 1989), p. 405.

16 George Orwell, *The Lion and the Unicorn: Socialism and the English Genius* (Penguin, 1992), p. 35.

17 Ibid., pp. 36–7.

18 Ibid., p. 96.

19 George Orwell, 'Not Counting Niggers', in *The Collected Essays, Journalism and Letters, vol. 1* (Penguin, 1970), p. 434.

20 George Orwell, 'My Country Right or Left', in *In Defence of English Cooking* (Penguin, 2005), p. 6.

21 George Orwell, 'Towards European Unity', in *The Collected Essays, Journalism and Letters, vol. 4* (Penguin, 1970), p. 425.

22 George Orwell, *Nineteen Eighty-Four* (Penguin, 1989), p. 5. Orwell wouldn't be the last person to mistake white Portland stone cladding or applied white render for the actual colour of 'glittering, white' concrete, which is of course in reality grey or brown.

23 Anthony Burgess, *1985* (Arrow, 1980), p. 21.

24 Ibid., p. 26.

25 Ibid., p. 29.

26 Ibid., p. 38.

27 Isaac Deutscher, '1984 – the Mysticism of Cruelty', in *Marxism, Wars and Revolutions: Essays from Four Decades* (Verso, 1984), p. 69. Given that – as he could not have known in his lifetime – Deutscher appeared on Orwell's little list submitted to the secret services of potential collaborators with a Red Army invasion of England, this is especially cutting. Seeing as Deutscher, a prominent and unrepentant Polish Trotskyist, would surely have been first against the wall in the event of a real invasion, the extent of Orwell's paranoia should be obvious.

28 See Raymond Williams, *Orwell* (Fontana, 1971), p. 51.

29 George Orwell, *The Road to Wigan Pier* (Penguin, 1988), pp. 140, 152.

30 Ibid., p. 157.

31 Orwell, *The Lion and the Unicorn*, p. 103.

32 Victor Silverman, *Imagining Internationalism in American and British Labor, 1939–49* (University of Illinois Press, 2000), p. 54.

33 Ibid., p. 55.

34 Ibid., p. 59.

35 Ibid., pp. 64–5.

36 Ibid., p. 75.

37 Ibid., p. 189.

38 Quoted in Christoph Grafe, *People's Palaces: Architecture, Culture and Democracy in Post-War Western Europe* (Architectura & Natura, 2014), p. 119.

39 Ibid., p. 125.

40 Ibid., p. 64.

41 Semmel, *Imperialism and Social Reform*, p. 250.

42 Robert Skidelsky, *Britain Since 1900 – A Success Story?* (Vintage, 2014), p. 260.

43 Foot, *Aneurin Bevan*, p. 363.

44 See Nicklaus Thomas-Symonds, *Nye: The Political Life of Aneurin Bevan* (IB Tauris, 2015).

45 Lynsey Hanley, *Estates: An Intimate History* (Granta, 2007), p. 81.

46 Jennie Lee, *My Life with Nye* (Penguin, 1981), p. 187.

47 For an interesting account of the Cranbrook estate and its vicissitudes, see the chapter on housing in James Meek's *Private Island* (Verso, 2014)

48 Thomas-Symonds, *Nye*, p. 105.

49 Foot, *Aneurin Bevan*, p. 590.

5. Building the Austerity City

1 Steen Eiler Rasmussen, *London: The Unique City* (Pelican, 1961), p. 215.

2 David Birkbeck and Julian Hart, *A New London Vernacular* (Urban Design London, 2015), p. 6.

Index